To Bea
With Affection,
Francesca
XOXO...

Reflections 'N Pink

on the Wings of Love

by

Francesca Iosca-Pagnin

ISBN: 1-55383-002-4

Cover design by Francesca Iosca-Pagnin
Cover layout by Dark Horse Studio
Cover photograph by Darlene Polachic
Formatting by Chris Polachic

Pin concept and design by Francesca Iosca-Pagnin
Artistic interpretation of pin concept by Rob Pagnin

Printed and bound in Canada by
Friesens
Altona, Manitoba

This book used 100% recycled paper.

DEDICATION

Thank you, Jesus. Thank you, Mary.

When I was an elementary school teacher, there was a Prayer Corner in my classroom. In the centre of the Prayer Corner was a picture of Jesus and Mary surrounded by decorations the children had made.

Every week I would choose a quote from the Bible and print it on coloured paper, and every morning we would begin our day with the quotation. The children loved to gesture when reciting from the Bible, hence gesturing became an integral part of our ritual during Religion Lessons. With arms stretched upward to heaven, and in solidarity, we would declare: "Here I am, Lord, I have come to do Your Will."

I hope and pray, Lord, that I, too, have done Your Will.

This book is dedicated to:

My parents, Vincenzo and Meluccia Iosca - Thank you for instilling values that have shaped me into who I am.

Roberto - Your love and support were instrumental in getting this book completed. Thank you for allowing me to soar on the wings of God's Love. I am blessed to have you in my life.

Rob and Cristina - May this book symbolize that there is always a positive aspect to anything life may throw your way. If you ask God for guidance, you will never get lost.

To Rosemarie - To my sister and private nurse, and to her family, Brent, Sarah and Mark, thanks for all the TLC.

The Reader - There is no end to what God can do for those who love Him. Thank you for sharing in my journey *'NPink.*

ACKNOWLEDGEMENTS

To Darlene Polachic - Your belief and sensitivity to the project made *Reflections 'NPink* possible. Thank you for allowing the Spirit of God to work through you in bringing this book to fruition.

To Irene Danaher - Through laughter and tears we made our way together through the breast cancer journey. Reading aloud to each other from the manuscript created more memories to be treasured. Thank you, dear friend.

To Judy Moneo, Alice Risling, Verna Carr, and Donalda Gerstmar - Thank you for taking time to read and offer suggestions for *Reflections 'NPink.*

To Carmela Amico - Your wisdom and guidance were timely. Thank you.

To Carmela Shearer - Thank you for caring enough to take me to Carmen. Without her, there quite simply would be no book.

To Bernard - With much appreciation for sharing your immense knowledge and talents in the service of others.

To Carmen - They say that one gets to heaven leaning on the arms of those you have helped here on earth. There will be many, many arms reaching out to you, Carmen. May God bless you as you continue with your ministry. With much love and gratitude, *thank you.*

PROLOGUE

When I was diagnosed with breast cancer in 1994, I knew that in order to survive I had to set an attainable, short-term goal. That goal was realized. 'Fighting Back Through Education' provided me with the vehicle to share my experience in the hope that it would help other women in the fight against this insidious disease known as breast cancer. I soon realized that taking a bad situation and turning it into something positive was helping to stimulate the healing process for me.

As further insurance, I set a long-term goal, something toward which I could work. That goal became the 1998 and 1999 Breast Cancer Walks, the first public-wide events and fundraisers for breast cancer in our city.

In 2000, my energies were turned to fundraising for a One-Stop Quick Diagnosis Breast Health Centre. Those plans had to be put on hold.

In 2001, I had a breast cancer recurrence. A visionary with the gift of healing hands was asked to pray for me. It was at this point that I became obsessed with the need to document and journal everything that was happening to me.

Keeping a journal was something new for me. I had never kept a diary in my life.

Along with all the medical and physical things that were occurring, my life was also undergoing a spiritual transformation.

Often, I would get up at 3:00 a.m. and work at the computer for hours, making sure the details of events were entered with clarity and accuracy. On many occasions, my husband Roberto would come down to make sure I was okay.

I knew that somehow this was a story that had to be shared. I realized the story of my journey could be a faith builder.

From that came the conviction that if such a book were written, it would become an invaluable gift for my children. Not only that, I thought, a successful book might generate funds that could be given to a worthy cause. I was certainly no stranger to fundraising, and I liked the idea of 'paying it forward'. If my book *really* sold, I wanted the money to be put back into the global community and into my own community which embraced me with open arms on so many occasions along my incredible journey.

The backtracking from 2001 is subsequential. The essence of my story is the spiritual aspect, and as I write this, I trust that God will show me each step I am supposed to take. I continue to pray for guidance.

Holy Spirit, open my lips and let my tongue pro-

claim Your praises.

Dear Jesus, I love you. Thank You for my life. Lead me, Lord, and I will follow.

But...terfly

Cancer has taken my hair...but
Cancer has given me the birth of transformation
  and wisdom.

Cancer has taken my eyebrows and eyelashes...but
Cancer has given me clarity of vision
  never imagined possible.

Cancer has taken many friends...but
Cancer has given me reaffirmed belief
  in the Resurrection.

Cancer has taken my vulnerability...but
Cancer has given me an instilled determination
  to win.
Cancer may take my body...but
Cancer will never claim my SPIRIT
  for it belongs to GOD.

Cancer can NEVER take away my ability to LOVE,
  the balm of true living.

Butterfly,

Francesca Iosca-Pagnin
(1997)

CHAPTER ONE

My Journey *'NPink* was launched in March of 1994. That was the year I was given a wake-up call--a jolt and a second chance to start my life anew. And when you are given a second chance at life, you shoot for the stars and soar on the wings of your dreams.

March 11, 1994, was the day the telephone call came to say that I had breast cancer. That became the day I donned permanent, yet invisible pink-tinted glasses which enabled me to look at life from a different perspective--my life in the pink, my *vie en rose*, my rebirth, an opportunity to seize life and make it count.

It was a Friday afternoon. I was in the kitchen with my family. We had had an early supper because Roberto, my husband, had to go back to work. He and our two children, Rob and Cristina, were busy cleaning up the dishes. When the telephone rang at 5:15, I answered.

It was my doctor.

"Francesca," she said, "your mammogram has come back and they've found something. We're pretty sure it's breast cancer."

No softening the blow. No leading up to it, or breaking the news gently. Just a blunt, matter-of-fact statement.

I was stunned. My legs felt as if they had turned to jelly. I sagged against the counter. "Are you sure?"

"Yes," she said calmly, "there is very little doubt. The mammogram shows what looks like a malignant tumour. You will have to see a specialist on Monday."

My first instinct was to protect my children, Rob and Cristina, who were 15 and 13 at the time. I cannot let this affect them, I thought.

My second instinct was to scream.

I hung up the phone, and stood for a moment, struggling desperately to regain my composure before going back to the kitchen, but my mind was in a turmoil.

How could this be? I was a healthy, active woman with a completely uneventful medical history: no appendicitis, no tonsillitis, very few colds. I lived a healthy lifestyle and cooked everything from scratch. I didn't smoke cigarettes and drank only an occasional glass of wine with dinner. I walked five kilometres every day. Even more important, there was no history of cancer in my family.

True, I had not been in the habit of doing regular breast examinations, but I hadn't thought there was any need.

Months earlier, by accident, I had discovered a pea-sized nodule in my left breast. I was lying on the bed with my hand on my breast, and my fingers encountered a very hard lump, like a sun-dried pea. It was located at the two o'clock position and was so close to my rib cage, I thought it might be a bump on the bone. It certainly didn't cross my mind that it was anything serious.

I showed the lump to Roberto and had him feel it. "What do you think?" I asked.

He agreed with me that it was probably nothing. "Just a bump on the chest wall," he guessed.

I dismissed the lump, mostly because I had too many other demands on my life at that moment to worry about it. There were piano, swimming, and dance lessons, soccer practice and school activities, not to mention the fact that I was the primary caregiver for my parents, aged 81 and 66, who were both very ill at the time. I had no time to get sick.

As it happened, it wasn't the lump in my breast that had prompted me to see my doctor. I had been experiencing severe cramping in my legs. Since I was already there, I asked her to check my left breast.

"You need a mammogram," she said.

This telephone call was my doctor informing me of the mammogram results.

Interestingly, the cramps in my legs disappeared on their own. In retrospect, I believe they were God's way of getting me to a doctor before the lump in my breast got any bigger.

Now the doctor was telling me the lump was malignant. I had cancer.

Breast cancer? Me? That hard, pea-sized nodule I had found was malignant? I hadn't thought it was anything to worry about. If only I had gone to the doctor sooner.

The dishes were finished when I returned to the kitchen, so I sent Rob and Cristina off to their rooms to do their homework. When they were safely out of earshot, I told Roberto what the doctor had said.

His reaction was complete disbelief.

"It can't be true," he said flatly. "You're the healthiest woman I know. You've never been sick a day in your life. They've made a mistake. They've mixed up your mammogram with some other woman's."

Oh, how I wished it were so.

Roberto co-owns the only Italian-owned restaurant in our city, and it was his turn to stay until the last customer of the evening was gone, which often turns out to be very late.

"Do you want me to stay home with you?" he inquired, giving me a kiss. "I can call Walter and he'll look after things at the restaurant tonight."

I shook my head. "You go. I'll be okay."

"Are you sure?"

"I'm sure."

I was forcing myself to sound calm and composed, but inside, I felt like a kettle ready to boil over. The words *breast cancer* had shaken me to the core of my being. I was filled with fear and panic. The moment Roberto left, I walked into the sound-proof swimming pool area off the kitchen and freaked out.

I was seized by a sense of utter desperation, but before the black, suffocating waves completely engulfed me, I ran to the phone and called my sister Rosemarie, who lives out of town.

Rosemarie didn't hesitate for a moment. "I'm leaving right now," she said. "I'm coming to be with you."

I hung up, and dialled my good friend Giuliana's number. By now I was sobbing uncontrollably. I don't even remember what I said, but within minutes Giuliana was at the door with three of her children: Remo, Dino, and Silvia. At their mother's suggestion, they took Rob and Cristina out so that Giuliana and I could be alone.

I don't know who called whom, but in remarkably short time Giuliana and two other friends, Valerie and Maria, and my sister Rosemarie were gathered in my family room. We tried bravely to deal with the medical news that had us all feeling shell-shocked. I recall wishing another friend, Judy, was with us, but she was out of town.

The five of us talked, and we cried.

After a while, a strange calm came over me. It seemed as if once I had gotten over the initial blow of realizing I had breast cancer, I became the strong one. My friends were still in a daze.

Maria was the first to notice my composure. She told me later: "You were not distraught; you weren't morbid. I couldn't believe how calm you were. I kept thinking: 'This is not happening. This is not real.' I began to talk to you about cabbage and how it is a can- cer-fighting food. I said: 'I'm going to make you some cabbage soup.' I needed a 'quick fix', something that would fix the problem now."

It was a typical reaction for Maria who is the man- ager of a cosmetic line. Her business-like persona wanted to address and rectify the issue immediately. Maria was also my walking buddy. For years, we walked five kilometres in sunshine, snow, sleet and rain. Feisty Maria, who comes from near Rome, Italy, was not going to take this attack on her friend sitting down.

Maria's observation was correct. Once I got control of myself, my perspective was: This has happened, now I have to deal with it. Thank God, I thought, I have a strong support system in my family and friends.

I was even able to joke with the girls about the fact that I had just bought some pretty new bras. "It's too bad," I said ruefully. "I may not need them now."

I may have seemed composed, but underneath, the raw truth of the diagnosis was only beginning to sink in. It hit me full force a couple of days later when Val- erie came over with the gift of a terra cotta roaster. Her idea was that I should incorporate roasted garlic into my diet. Garlic is a powerful antioxidant, and Valerie believed it would be good for my health.

It was that afternoon that the full impact of my di- agnosis hit. I recall cradling the roaster in my arms and breaking into tears. "I don't want to die, Val," I sobbed. "I have so much to live for."

I knew very little about breast cancer or its treatments, although I had heard about mastectomies or surgical removal of a breast. I was very relieved to learn that, in my case, a lumpectomy would be enough to remove the nodule in my breast.

The surgery was scheduled for March 24, 1994, two weeks after the diagnosis. Originally, it was scheduled for sometime in April, but I knew I could not wait that long. I phoned my doctor and told her that I had never made any unnecessary impositions on the health care system, but if they didn't operate sooner than April, they would be dealing with me on more than one health-related issue! Fortunately, she spoke to someone about my urgent circumstances, and my date was pushed ahead.

I had asked for a private room, but when the time came for me to enter hospital, none was available. I had to share a room with three other women. Directly across from me was a woman named Linda. We immediately became friends.

Linda was a courageous, smiling thirty-two-year-old with a husband and three young sons who were eagerly awaiting her return home. Linda had cancer of the liver. She had been in hospital for a long time and had undergone numerous extensive surgeries. The hardest thing for her was being away from her children. She missed them terribly, and was especially worried about her youngest two who were twins. I couldn't help but admire her spirit. She had been through so much, yet she was still optimistic about getting well and going home.

Following my lumpectomy surgery, a private room came available.

"Please don't go," Linda begged.

I thanked the nurse and told her I had no intention of moving. The other three in the room might have had second thoughts about having me stay if they had known the room would soon resemble a mini-market with people coming and going with gifts and flowers.

After I was released from hospital, Linda and I kept in touch through regular phone calls. I will never forget the telephone conversation we had prior to her passing away. She had called to tell me her family was planning a big reunion which was going to take place at the hospital in Spiritwood, Saskatchewan, where she was staying. Linda was ecstatic as she told me that her sisters had bought a new dress for her to wear, and that they were going to 'doll her up' for the party. I recall desperately fighting back tears because I knew that Linda must have very little time left. That conversation ended with best wishes for a great gathering.

The next time I received a phone call from Spiritwood it was Linda's husband, Bill, informing me of her death. Linda died a year after we met. I will never forget her infectious laughter. *Thank you, God, for bringing Linda into my life.*

My sister Rosemarie came to the hospital every day and always stayed until late at night. For me, the older sister, watching Rose take over was a total role reversal. I knew she had loved her work nursing the elderly in a seniors' residence, but I had never seen her in action. She was a natural. Rosemarie was generous in giving Linda lots of TLC. She was extremely kind and caring, giving Linda back massages, rubbing her legs, and washing and curling her hair.

Linda loved my nightshirt, so I asked Rose to go and buy one for her. She was delighted when she opened the gift, a green and blue floral nightshirt. "We can be the Bobbsey Twins," I quipped.

Rosemarie had left her little son Mark, who had just turned two, and seven-year-old Sarah with her sister-in-law, Lucille, so she could be with me. I didn't learn until much later how deeply my illness affected her. When Rosemarie would go for coffee with Giuliana and Maria, they would literally have to hold her upright.

My good friends Giuliana and Maria also came everyday to visit. Giuliana was so distraught that she would take refuge in the hospital chapel where she would cry and pray, then put on a brave face to come and see me. Afterward, she would go back to the chapel. On one occasion, at my mother's home, Rosemarie walked in on Giuliana and my mother crying together. Neither could console the other.

I had no idea all this was happening behind the scenes.

The morning of my surgery, when I met the surgeon, I told him that I had prayed for him and confirmed one more time that he would only be doing a lumpectomy, not taking off the whole breast.

Waking up after surgery, I remember checking to see if my body was still whole. I was grateful to find my left breast had not been removed. It was some time, however, before I had the courage to look at the 25 stitches that were now a part of my new reality.

I came through the lumpectomy confidently, buoyed by a strong and positive frame of mind. My surgeon was optimistic; given my age and the size of the tumour, he said, my prognosis was good.

Psychologically, I was doing fine. My sister remarked on it. "It seems bizarre and surreal," she said. "You have all these flowers around, and you're so cheerful, you could be in here having a baby, not being treated for breast cancer."

The surgeon came to see me the morning after surgery.

"You look as if you should be eating steak, not jello," he quipped. He was referring to the fact that I was dressed in a rose and gold silk nightshirt that I had purchased specifically for my stay in hospital because I refused to wear the drab hospital gowns. My doctor had no idea how much effort it had taken me that morning to dress in my own nightshirt. It seemed a way of regaining some control over my life.

The surgeon paid me another visit the morning I was to be discharged. He wanted to discuss my pathology report. It showed that three of the nine lymph nodes removed at the time of the lumpectomy surgery were affected. That meant follow-up treatment at the

Cancer Clinic would be necessary.

Linda, Rosemarie, and I discussed the pathology report after the surgeon left. It seemed fairly clear-cut to me: I would have the chemotherapy, I said confidently, and I would be fine.

A nurse, who happened to be in the room at the time, overheard the conversation. "When it's gone to the nodes," she declared gloomily, shaking her head, "it's not good."

She may have thought she was being helpful, but she had just pronounced a Doomsday sentence for me. I felt as if I had been kicked in the stomach. For the first time since my ordeal began, I was robbed of hope.

I pulled the curtains around my bed like the walls of a cocoon. It was a sterile cocoon. Roberto had taken home one cartful of my belongings the night before, and Rosemarie had loaded everything else onto another cart ready for departure. Housekeeping had already stripped the bed down to the plastic mattress. I felt as stark and stripped as my surroundings.

I sat there alone, stiff and numb, as the realization sank in. My God, I thought, I could die from this.

I had never entertained the thought of dying before. And why would I? I was young. I had a family who needed me. I had been so confident I would recover from this. Was I wrong?

My body was paralyzed, my mind blank. I felt as if I were in a coma. I didn't even hear my sister Rosemarie outside the curtains, rebuking the nurse.

"That was uncalled for," she said.

The nurse shrugged. "Your sister needs to know the truth about her condition."

"Who made you her doctor?" Rosemarie shot back.

At that point, the nurse in charge of my care for the day came into the room to say good-bye and wish me well. She discovered me behind the curtains, visibly shaken.

I told her what had taken place.

Rosemarie joined us and we all agreed that I should talk to my surgeon again before leaving.

As we waited for the doctor to return, I was deeply despondent. Rosemarie tried her best to comfort me.

During the wait, the Head Nurse came by to see how I was doing. Seeing my anguished state, she persuaded me to tell her why I was so upset.

When I was finished, she told Rosemarie to leave the room. Her reason was that the doctor would want to see me alone. Rosemarie knew it was more likely because word had gotten back to the nursing station about how she had rebuked the nurse, and she was now perceived as a threat.

Reluctantly, Rosemarie left.

Eventually the doctor came, with the Head Nurse (whom I had not seen until that day) glued to his side. I wish now I had asked her to leave.

The doctor listened carefully to what I had to say. When he learned my reason for wanting to see him again, he became very upset. "There are many factors that affect a person's recovery," he declared. "What does she [the nurse] know?"

A couple of times, the Head Nurse tried to inter-ject, but the doctor ignored her. With treatment, he as-sured me, there was no reason why I should not main-tain my initial optimism.

I thanked him very much for coming again. I was grateful to be in his care.

I was also eager to accept his encouraging progno-sis. I wanted so much to regain some control over my life which had, in two short weeks, been turned com-pletely upside down. I loved my life and wanted every-thing to be back to normal. I couldn't wait to get home.

While I waited for Rosemarie to come back to the room, I prayed desperately for God's Divine interven-tion. "I need Your help," I cried. "I cannot do this without You. I cannot do this on my own. Jesus of Di-vine Mercy, fill me with Your love. Jesus of Divine Mercy, fill me with Your peace."

Alone in the curtained enclosure, I clung to the pink rosary that had been given to me when I was in my early twenties by a family friend, a little old Italian lady, Nonnina Rosa. Never having known my grand-mother, I thought of Nonnina Rosa as my grandmother. She had brought the rosary back from a trip to Italy. One bead was missing, but I didn't mind. I cherished the rosary and when I prayed it, whenever I came to the place of the missing bead, I would smile and recall with affection the endearing little old lady who gave it to me.

A few days earlier, a friend, Arlene, had come to visit. At first I was suitably polite, thanking her for the beautiful flowers she had brought, but all the while wondering where in the sheets and blankets I had lost my pink rosary. Finally, out of sheer frustration, I told Arlene that I needed to find my rosary in order to enjoy her visit. With her help, we soon located the precious pink beads.

My rosary had become my security and my safeguard, but now not even it could relieve my despair and desolation. I felt painfully helpless.

Where was Rosemarie? Roberto would be coming soon to take me home. I was fully dressed, but I didn't have any shoes. I needed shoes. Without them, I felt even more vulnerable.

I walked toward the elevators in search of Rosemarie, hugging myself. The thought kept running through my mind: 'My God, I could die from this.'

I tried to shift my thoughts to other things, but couldn't. My brain seemed stuck on a one-way track that was heading toward complete hopelessness.

Finally I saw Rosemarie coming toward me with the cart filled with my belongings.

"Roberto is here," she said. "He's waiting for us."

"Did he bring my shoes?"

He hadn't. I would have to go home in slippers. As I look back now, I realize why I had so desperately wanted my shoes: when one dies, one's mortal remains no longer requires shoes.

In the elevator, I drew a couple of very deep breaths, hoping somehow to dispel the anxiety that was overwhelming me. The breathing didn't work, but something else was in store that would bolster my courage and spark the embers of hope that had all but burned out.

When the elevator doors opened on the main floor, the first person I saw was Comare Irene, a family friend. When she saw me, she smiled. Her effervescent, ear-to-ear smile at that precise moment meant more to me than any words she could ever have spoken.

We embraced, and she assured me in our familiar Italian dialect that she knew I was going to be fine. I don't remember what I said to her, but I cherished her words of encouragement and hugged them to my heart.

I knew very little about cancer, but that was about to change. I immediately began reading and researching as much as I could to learn what I didn't know about the disease.

I discovered that all of us have cancer cells, but it is when there is an irregular growth of these abnormal cells that a person is said to have cancer. In other words, cancer occurs when body cells go haywire and cannot stop reproducing themselves. They are dangerous because they rob normal body cells of space and nourishment.

Through my reading, I learned that breast cancer calls for either a mastectomy (the surgical removal of the breast) or a lumpectomy (the surgical removal of the suspicious localized mass or lesion). With both procedures, the lymph nodes in the immediate area are also removed to determine whether or not the cancer has spread. The function of the lymph system is to provide fluid to body tissues and to carry waste away from the cells. Lymph nodes are the sieves that filter out the lymphatic system.

The procedure performed on me was a lumpec-tomy. The hard pea-sized lump had grown to the size of a dollar coin and had begun to take on the contours of the breast. In the process, it had lost the hard shape that made it suspicious. This placed me at a Stage II of breast cancer.

The lump and the lymph nodes were sent to a pa-thology lab to determine if the cancer had spread to the lymph nodes. Because it had, chemotherapy treatment was prescribed.

Radiation therapy and chemotherapy are the most widely used cancer treatments. Radiation therapy uses high energy x-rays to zap out or destroy the cancer cells. This treatment lasts a few minutes each day and is most commonly used when the lymph nodes are not affected. The side effects are less severe than with chemotherapy which treats the disease with drugs that are administered intravenously. This cocktail of drugs destroys cancer cells by interfering with their growth or by preventing their further reproduction. The intrave-nous process can last a short time or take many hours.

The side effects of chemotherapy are partial or complete loss of hair, nausea, vomiting, diarrhea, and extreme fatigue. Some recipients become violently ill.

The type of cancer I had warranted chemotherapy, and one month later, I arrived at the Cancer Clinic for the first of twelve treatments. They were given in six cycles of two weeks per cycle with a rest period of two weeks between cycles.

As Roberto and I walked into the Cancer Clinic, I was disconcerted by the sound of children's laughter. Where am I? I asked myself. Am I in a park? Why are there children here?

At that moment, another reality hit me. I realized this cancer thing had put me in a whole new ball park where I had never played before. There were children here because they had cancer. The thought of my own children fighting this disease hit me like a wash of ice water. Thank God it's me with the cancer, I said, and not my children.

Roberto and I met with my oncologist, or cancer specialist. We discussed the various chemotherapy regimens and I was offered a choice of chemotherapies. Since I knew nothing about any of them, I asked bluntly: "If this were your pathology/cancer report, which of the therapies would you choose?"

"In your situation," she replied, "I would choose the more aggressive chemo, adriamycin." I would later learn that particular chemo treatment was known as 'The Red Devil'.

What resonates to this day about my first meeting with the oncologist was the fact that she spent most of the time talking about and trying to recruit me for a research study that was being conducted on a drug called tamoxifen. The drug was being tested on women whose cancer was estrogen receptor negative, as mine was.

I felt I needed to know more about the different

chemotherapies before I made any decisions, and after some research, I opted for the standard conventional chemotherapy CMF (cyclophosphamide, methotrexate, and 5-fluorouracil) because it had been tried and extensively tested.

A week later, I was seated in a cushy, comfortable, LazyBoy-type chair in a room overlooking the beautiful South Saskatchewan River. I took a deep breath as the nurse inserted the IV needle into my arm.

I looked up at Roberto who had come with me. There were tears in his eyes. He turned away to the window to hide them.

I told the nurse I wished to meditate and asked that no one bother me for the hour and a half it would take for the chemical cocktail to drain into my veins.

No one did.

The memory that lingers most vividly in my mind of that chemotherapy lab is the distinctive medicinal smell that permeated it. The odour bit into my nostrils, and I thought it would drive me mad on that first visit. For every visit afterward, I took along a scented sachet which I held near my nose and imagined that I was in a field of lavender instead of the chemo lab.

After my first chemotherapy treatment, I felt dizzy, displaced, and somewhat nauseous.

When I got home, I was welcomed by two very frightened-looking children who had the table all set for dinner. I tried to eat, but during the meal the nausea got so bad, I had to excuse myself and go upstairs. On the way, I grabbed a box of crackers.

I sat next to the toilet and went through a couple of dry heaves. Then breathing deeply, I began to nibble on the crackers.

I kept thinking about how frightened Rob and Cristina looked. More than anything, I wanted to go back downstairs to reassure them.

Putting on my headband, I splashed my face with cold water and said: "Damn it, this is not going to get the best of me. I simply refuse to let this get the best of me."

I went downstairs and had dinner with my family. I never had a problem with the chemotherapy treatments again.

Fortunately, I had very few side effects outside of some hair loss, my eyebrows and eyelashes disappearing, and bouts of fatigue. All in all, I considered myself very lucky.

Today, I see it was not luck at all. I had always been a spiritual person, but this painful experience was deepening my faith and my dependence on God. My spirituality would become a vital force that would play a major role in my recovery.

About this time, I began reading a book my family doctor gave me. It was entitled '*LOVE, MEDICINE, AND MIRACLES: Lessons Learned About Self-Healing From a Surgeon's Experience With Exceptional Patients*' by Dr. Bernie Siegel, M.D. In the book, Siegel offered meditation and visualization techniques as a means of creating a self-healing environment.

Imagery that comes through meditation is ultimately influenced by past and present experiences which become a foundation for the imagery one receives during meditation.

Following the suggestions in the book, I began to visualize myself with an Inner Guide, a life-sized white rabbit who walked upright and wore a bright blue vest. I named him Happy.

Every time I prayed, meditated, or went for a chemotherapy treatment, I would settle back in the easy chair, close my eyes, and visualize Happy waiting for me at the bottom of a flight of ten moss-covered, concrete steps that seemed to be carved out of a mountain. As I descended the steps, I counted backwards.

Happy led me through the autumn woods. We always walked on the same gravel road until we came to a fork. We would turn right and continue on until we came to a house in a clearing. Inside the house, I climbed a flight of stairs that led to a healing room on the left. There, I would receive healing treatment to rid my body of any further cancer invasion. There was always a doctor in the room, someone wearing white.

I saw myself stepping out of my skin. I would take my skin and give it a vigorous shake on the balcony to get rid of the cancer. Then I visualized any cancer cells still attached to my body being destroyed, one by one, as the wind blew them off. (The derivative for this particular imagery is the fact that I have a clothesline on our balcony where I often hang out our garments for airing.) I then climbed back into my skin and proceeded to a beautiful room across the hall.

In this room, I saw myself as a little girl of about five years old, playing with two friends. There was a bed in the room, and at the foot of it, a little table set for tea parties. Lovingly, I embraced the child that was me, and memories of a past time filled my mind.

When I left that room, I became an adult again and proceeded down the stairs to the main floor of the house and out the door. Happy was always waiting for me at the edge of the clearing to lead me back through the woods. Any questions I had were answered by an Inner Voice.

Happy and I always shared a hug before parting. Then I ascended the same ten steps. At the top, I would turn and look down at Happy, then wave good-bye until the next time when he would once again be waiting for me at the bottom of the steps.

The format of my visualization never changed. To this day, I cannot see the house I entered, but I can describe the rooms in detail.

When the chemotherapy was finished, my oncologist recommended radiation treatment as further insurance against the recurrence of cancer. That took another month.

And then there was the tamoxifen study.

By now, I had researched tamoxifen and found out a number of things. Cancer is diagnosed as 'ER (estrogen receptor) positive' or 'ER negative'. Tamoxifen works best on women whose cancer cells develop in the presence of estrogen (as happens in estrogen-receptor positive breast cancer). For these women, tamoxifen acts as a block against the estrogen hormone. However, for ER negative patients like me, the benefits were very dubious because the cancer was not caused by the estrogen hormone. There was also a risk of developing uterine and endometrial cancer with tamoxifen.

The tamoxifen study I had been told about was recruiting ER negative women across Canada. One group would be given tamoxifen; the remainder would be given a placebo, or sugar pill. No one would know what they were taking. At the end of the study, results would be examined to see if the ER-negative group taking tamoxifen had derived any significant benefit compared to the group taking the placebo. In effect, we would be the guinea pigs.

Was I interested in being part of this study?

I have never been someone who was content to sit back and just endure. Being a teacher by profession, and an analytical and pro-active sort by nature, I had already embarked on a program of information and education on the subject of breast cancer. I felt I needed to do something constructive to make sense of what had happened to me.

I wrote a proposal entitled *Fighting Back Through Education* and presented it to the Cancer Society, the local Public Health Board, and the Catholic and Public Boards of Education in Saskatoon, Saskatchewan, where I live. With the approval and endorsement of all those agencies, I began a schedule of public presentations on the subject of breast cancer. The honoraria I received were donated to cancer initiatives.

On one occasion, I left the Cancer Clinic after a treatment and headed directly to Sion High School to make a presentation to its female students. On the way, I remember thinking about the research study. If no one is willing to take part in these studies, I thought, we are never going to find out what needs to be known. That could affect the girls I am going to speak to today. It could someday affect my own daughter. I realized then and there, that if I was going to be making these presentations on breast cancer, I had better be prepared to walk the walk and talk the talk.

Sidelining my fear regarding the possibility that tamoxifen could cause uterine or endometrial cancer in ER negative women like me, I contacted my oncologist to say I would participate in the trials.

And so, when my regimen of chemotherapy and radiation was finished, I began faithfully popping a tamoxifen/placebo pill every day for the next five years and prayed that I was not harming myself by taking them.

At the time, I had no idea if I was taking tamoxifen or a placebo. By accident, I found out after the study was complete that I had, indeed, been on tamoxifen.

I had many opportunities to speak to the public about breast cancer. By mid-1997, after much networking and partnering with individuals and organizations within the community, I was ready to bring the first public-wide event for breast cancer to Saskatoon. The fundraiser walks of 1998 and 1999 were a huge success and unprecedented in terms of money raised, sponsors acquired, and participants. Some of the funds from the 1998 Walk were used to buy an apheresis machine for stem cell transplants in Saskatoon. It was a great boon. No longer did women who needed stem cell transplants have to travel out of the province for their treatment.

The people of Saskatchewan were outstanding in their support for breast cancer. The walk committee was extremely proud of its accomplishments. We did what we set out to do: raise breast cancer awareness and fund the apheresis machine.

Now my imagination was captured by a bigger dream: the idea of raising funds to establish a One-Stop Quick Diagnosis Breast Health Centre in Saskatoon. Such centres do in days what most clinics accomplish in weeks.

This new goal filled me with fire and enthusiasm. The cancer had been treated; my life was back to normal once again, and I had a worthy cause into which I could pour my energy and my fundraising skills.

On top of that, a new millennium was approaching, and to me, it seemed symbolic of renewed hope and optimism, and the new lease on life I had been given. I had no idea my life was approaching a critical crossroads.

CHAPTER TWO

As Christmas of 1999 approached, my focus was on all the fun and festive preparations that go with it. Often, during that season, I found myself thinking how good life was. I had a fantastic husband, two great children, a stable life, and a strong and colourful heritage of which I was justifiably proud.

I was born in the sunny south of Italy in the small village of Pietrapertosa. Pietrapertosa is located in the Basilicata region of Italy, roughly seven hours by car from Rome. I say 'roughly seven hours' because anyone who has travelled in Italy knows very well there is no speed limit, at least not a speed limit to which anyone adheres. On my initial return visits to my homeland, travelling on the roads by car made me feel like I was on some wild ride at the fair.

Pietrapertosa is a charming village of about two thousand people, carved out of the side of a mountain 1088 metres (3579 feet) above sea level. The cobblestone roads of this picturesque village are so narrow that only small cars can navigate safely through the streets with no risk to the vehicle.

In 1999, as our family made plans for a visit to Italy, Roberto arranged to rent a mid-sized car in Germany. However, when we landed in Munich, the car he had reserved was unavailable, so we were given a larger one at no extra cost. The added room was nice, but navigating the vehicle through Pietrapertosa was no easy task.

Roberto managed to park the car near the home of my relatives. Any other manoeuvers proved to be large-scale productions. Just backing it up required the assistance of one, and preferably two people acting as guides. It was my job to keep an eye out and see that Roberto did not back the shiny new Opel Vectra into the massive concrete stairs that led to the home of my cousin.

When Roberto was parking the car on our arrival, I was too busy visiting to give the necessary guidance. As a result, the back end of the rental car received more than just a kiss from the cement stairway. I was never asked to navigate again and the incident of the car became an ongoing joke at my expense. The only time we moved the car again was the morning of our departure.

The day we left was in stark contrast to our joyous fun-filled arrival, and rightly so. The morning we were to leave, the whole family agreed to meet in Pietrapertosa's main piazza, on the edge of which stands my cousin Francesca's and her husband Rocco's house. Roberto, accompanied by Rob and Cristina, carefully manoeuvered the Vectra to the piazza, while my cousins Rinuccia, Giuseppina, Francesca, and I walked armin-arm down a street that was too narrow for any car.

We walked silently, clutching each other's arms tightly. I continually turned back to have one last look. Through the arched passageway, I glanced down at the court where Rinuccia's and Giuseppina's homes were. How different their lives were from mine, I thought.

When we got to the piazza, all our family and friends were gathered, including Rocco, a kind and gentle soul who took me aside. "When you were small, I was engaged to your cousin," he told me. "Do you remember how when I teased you, you used to stick out your tongue at me and run?" We chuckled together at the recollection.

Then Rocco led me to the garage and around to a space that was partitioned off from the rest of the garage by a wall. "I have a special gift for you," he said, and added: "*Ti accompagna con la Madonna*--I will send you off with the Madonna."

Rocco brought out his violin and tucked it under his chin. "Forgive me if I am a little rusty," he said. "I haven't played in years."

He lifted the bow to the violin and soon the magnificent strains of Schubert's 'Ave Maria' filled the little space. The exquisite sound brought everyone from the piazza to the door of the garage. There were tears in everyone's eyes.

We all embraced one more time. No words were spoken. Each of us was absorbed in the magical moment we had just shared.

As we made our way to the autostrada, Roberto, Rob, Cristina and I knew this would be a memory we would always treasure.

Visiting family and friends who live so far away is always like a double-edged sword. One is happy to arrive, but filled with sadness when the time comes to say *'Arrivederci--*'Til we see each other again'. I have come to realize that in life one can only appreciate and understand joy when one has experienced and known sadness.

My paternal grandparents were well-off financially. They lived in the village and ran a big farm on the outskirts of Pietrapertosa. Large herds of sheep and goats grazed on their land, and there were also olive groves, vineyards, and wheat fields, as well as orchards with apple, pear, cherry, fig, and chestnut trees. A huge vegetable garden was my grandmother's pride and joy, and in the centre of the garden was a fountain fed by an underground spring. The fountain was christened La Fontana Del Signore--the Fountain of the Lord.

Walking on the farm, or anywhere in the village, for that matter, was always an adventure because it involved extreme ascents and descents. On a visit in 1971, I remember going to the orchard where I ate delicious ripe cherries right off the tree. The vista from the sloped orchard was breathtaking. The old farm house was still standing at the time.

My grandmother Francesca and grandfather Vito Rocco Iosca, along with their family of seven children, farmed and ran the local store which was called Il Magazzino. It was located across the street from where my grandparents lived.

In the store, one could find cheeses, olive oil, grapes, wine, and wheat that was purchased and taken to the village mill to be ground. The local people gathered at Il Magazzino to exchange or barter services for goods. The use of currency was virtually non-existent in Pietrapertosa, so my grandparents became rich in possessions.

Grandmother (Nonna) Francesca was known for her kindness. She never turned anyone away. At a wedding some years ago, I had the pleasure of meeting Signora Minichina, a lady from the Tuscany region of Italy who lived in Pietrapertosa at one time. As a young woman, she was often at my Nonna's home. She recounted a time when she was having dinner with my grandmother. A young woman came to the door regarding a business matter. My grandmother immediately whisked her inside and insisted she join them for dinner. Signora Minichina noticed that during the meal, the young woman would take a few bites, then hide some of her food discreetly in her apron. Grandmother must have noticed, too, and guessed the reason, because she mentioned casually that she had prepared a box of food for the young woman to take home to her child. I was delighted to hear what a gracious and generous individual my grandmother was, and to realize how profoundly and practically she touched the lives of the people in her village.

My father, Vinçenzo (Vinny) Iosca, was from a family of seven children, five boys and two girls. The youngest sibling, Michele, died when he was twelve. That left my father as the youngest. Nonna Francesca never got over the death of her little son Michele.

When Grandfather passed away, my father was in his thirties and still a bachelor. My father apparently enjoyed being footloose and fancy-free and I have been told he was quite the ladies' man. I never thought of my father in this way, though I must admit the few photos we have of him as a young man show a very handsome fellow. I have often wished the photographs were in colour so they could show my father's fantastic hazel-green eyes.

Following Grandfather's death, Grandmother Francesca brought my father's bachelor life to an abrupt halt. She informed him that she had found him the prefect wife, a girl by the name of Meluccia Santamauro.

Unlike my father, my mother Meluccia came from a poor family. Her mother, Vinna Rosa, died shortly after Mom was born. Her father, Donata, died when she was twelve, which left the family of eight, four girls and four boys, obliged to pull together in order to survive on a farm that was located some distance from Pietrapertosa. My mother was the youngest in the family; her brother Ciccilo became the head of the Santamauro household.

A story my mother tells always tugs at my heart. It was harvest time on the farm and the older sisters had prepared dinner for the men working in the fields. The neighbours knew of the Santamauro family's struggle just to survive, and many had turned out to help with the harvest. My mother was four years old at the time and could not be left in the house by herself.

The fields being harvested were a half hour's walk from the farm, so my Aunt Raffaela, with my mother in tow, set out with the food for the hungry men. With her right hand, she steadied the cauldron of stew she was carrying on her head; with her left hand, she held onto my mother.

Along the way, Mother tripped and fell, cutting her head. Aunt Raffaela had to make a quick decision. Should she let go of the dinner, or let go of her little sister?

My mother fondly recalls her older sister's dilemma: "What was poor distraught Raffaela to do? The harvest help must be fed. Times were tough. We were eight motherless children trying to do the best we could in spite of the situation in which we found ourselves." Raffaela solved the problem by setting the cauldron safely on the ground and then taking care of her little sister's bleeding forehead.

I have had the pleasure of getting to know my Aunt Raffaela who is still a spirited, fun-loving woman.

My mother learned to cook under the guidance and supervision of her three older sisters. At the age of twelve, she was baking bread by herself. Rob and Cristina still maintain their grandmother's bread could win prizes.

It was as a result of errands to the village that my

mother Meluccia met my grandmother, and my father's fate was forever sealed.

After a year of courtship which included a six month engagement, my mother and father were married on October 18, 1948. I was born the following year. A few months after my birth, Nonna Francesca passed away.

I never met my grandmother, my namesake. I wish I had. Perhaps that is why I absorb every story about her with great joy and appreciation.

When my cousin Angela, who lives in Rome, was planning a Christmas trip to Pietrapertosa to visit her aunts and cousins, I asked her to pay a visit to Zia Rosina and find out everything she could about our grandmother. Zia Rosina's husband worked on my grandfather's farm, and Zia Rosina spent her days helping Grandmother run the house and Il Magazzino. Zia Rosina, her husband, and two children, Angelina and Nicola, shared many dinners in my grandmother's house, and became dear friends of the family.

In 1999, after hounding relatives for any keepsakes of my grandmother Francesca, my Mom remembered she had a pair of baby sheets that Grandmother Francesca embroidered for my crib. I was overjoyed when I saw those little white sheets, even though they were somewhat discoloured with age. On each corner, my grandmother had embroidered a butterfly. I found this a truly amazing coincidence. I have always been fascinated by the transformation of the ugly caterpillar into a splendid butterfly and have come to cherish the butterfly as a special personal symbol.

In 1950, my father left Italy for America in search of a better life. Two brothers and two sisters had already immigrated to New York.

My father often described the day he made his decision to leave. He had been running the farm and handling the affairs of the family since his father's death. On this particular day, he was out in the field. He took the hoe, planted it firmly in the ground, looked to the heavens and declared: "Enough." Then he proceeded back to the village where he found his brother Nicola and informed him of his intentions to leave.

My mother had always known of Dad's dream, but it had become even more important to him after I was born. Uncle Nicola was left to run the family business.

Dad did not know it then, but he would soon find out that what he had in Pietrapertosa was indeed the good life.

At the time of his application, the Italian Department of Immigration told Dad that Canada was accepting applicants, and that Saskatoon, Saskatchewan, in the middle of the country, needed populating. So that is where he ended up. Five years later, my mother and I joined him in this place with the strange-sounding name: Saskatoon.

After Grandmother died, Mother and I had continued to live in her house until the time was 'right' and my father had made the necessary arrangements for us to join him in Canada. For my father, the 'right' time meant when he had saved enough money to buy a house.

Unfortunately, my recollections of the first five years of my life in Pietrapertosa are limited. I remember going to kindergarten and seeing a large turtle on the cobblestone road on the way to school. The kindergarten was run by nuns. I have a recollection of having to put our heads down on cold desks which were made of a soft, shiny, silver metal.

Snow was unusual in Pietrapertosa, and when there was a snowfall, I remember the sweet taste of the slush that my cousins Rinuccia, Giuseppina, and Francesca made out of the freshly fallen snow.

My favourite memory is the breakfasts that my mother would prepare. I would have a slice of sopressata on homemade bread and a bit of wine to wash it down. My mother insists to this day that those little sips of wine were good for my health and did me no harm.

My mother tells me that since my father was not in Italy with us, everybody, relatives and friends included, felt they needed to spoil me--which they did. They called me 'La Principessa'.

The day of our final departure from Pietrapertosa was one of mixed emotions for my mother. While she was happy we were going to be reunited with my father, she was also very sad to be leaving all our family behind. At the farewell gathering, I was propped up on a chair to sing a song the nuns had taught me. *"Terra straniera quanta malinconia..."* The song was about someone who longs for their beloved homeland. My mother tells me that prior to leaving, I often went around singing the song which never failed to move my Uncle Nicola to tears. According to Mother, the farewell was as poignant as it was emotional.

My memory of the plane ride over is vague. However, I do recall clearly that when we landed in New York, we had to stay overnight in a hotel. Our room faced a huge neon light that could be seen flashing on and off, even with the drapes drawn. For a five-year-old child from a quaint mountain village, looking out over the vast metropolis of New York City must have been quite a culture shock. My mother wondered exactly where on earth my father had gone and how much longer it would take for us to reach our destination.

My father had endured many hardships during his first five years alone in Canada. He often told us how harsh he found the winters and how he longed for the warmth of the Italian sun. Dad would recall how he was always hungry, and that no matter how much he ate, he never felt satisfied. He missed the cuisine from home. Many times, Dad wondered if he had made the right choice in leaving a comfortable way of life for something completely unknown, but pride kept him determined to stay and carve out a life for himself in this new country of Canada.

My father was a pioneer, one of the first Italian immigrants to come to Saskatoon. He worked as a hired hand on several farms before he learned the art and trade of laying terrazzo floors, and he was proud of his work. Many of the floors in Saskatchewan display my father's craftsmanship. He especially enjoyed working on floors that had interesting mosaic patterns in them. There are a number of buildings in Saskatoon where my father's floors are still being buffed and shined to their original splendour. My many visits to Royal University Hospital were made just a little easier knowing I was walking on floors my dad had installed.

Dad, thank you for teaching me the meaning of integrity, honesty, and the dignity of an honest day's work. Grazie, Papà.

The first obstacle we encountered in Canada was the language. My mother claims the first English words I learned were: 'Shut up'. But before long, I was the translator for Mom who initially had a very difficult time learning English.

At school I was eager to assimilate and integrate into my new environment. I vividly remember begging my mother to take out the tiny gold earrings I had worn since birth. In Southern Italy, it was customary to have the ears of female children pierced immediately after birth. In Canada, none of the other girls wore earrings, and I didn't want to be any different. (Unfortunately, the woman who pierced my ear lobe had poor aim. As a result, I have one ear lobe pierced higher than the other, so wearing some types of earrings is virtually impossible.)

Another point of contention with my mother was the silk ribbons she made me wear in a huge bow on top of my head. She would say: "Francesca, one day you will understand...one day you will understand."

When the teachers pared down my name from Francesca to Frances, that was fine by me. In fact, it was great. I wanted desperately to blend in. However, when it was reduced even further to 'Fran' by one teacher with whom I would work years later, it was not so fine. I hated being called Fran. My mother found it rather amusing because she had felt the same way about my being called Frances. Being an immigrant who didn't know the language made her feel inadequate and inferior. Who was she, after all, to correct the teachers?

Another custom of Southern Italy is to name the firstborn after the father's side of the family. I was named after my father's mother Francesca, but it wasn't until I entered university and came to my senses that I consciously took back my given name.

I finally understand, Mom. It took a while, but better late than never. I am proud to be Italian-Canadian. They say one should never forget their origins. I never have. My roots and heritage have shaped me into the person I am today and keep me focused on who I want to become tomorrow.

Because of the way my name is written, I often have to explain that in the written Italian language there is no 'ch' digraph, although there is in the actual pronunciation. As a result, the verbal form of my name takes on many variations. Most of the time it is pronounced without the 'ch', which gives it Russian overtones. Still, I am definitely happy to have reclaimed my name, no matter how it is pronounced.

At first, my parents and I lived in the basement of a

Polish/Italian home. We were given two temporary rooms: a kitchen and a bedroom. Upon entering the basement area, because there was no door, one could look right into the tiny room that was our kitchen. For privacy, Mom made a curtain to separate the kitchen from the bedroom which the three of us shared.

Dad was often apologetic for the accommodations. He should have waited another year or two, he said, before having us come. By then he would have had enough money saved to buy us a house of our own. Mother kept reassuring him that it was better that we were all together, and that someday we would have our own home. Secretly, I think, she yearned for the life she had enjoyed while living with my grandmother Francesca.

One incident I will never forget became the catalyst, the straw that broke the camel's back, and precipitated the move to a place of our own. It happened during the summer. My parents were helping the landlords weed the garden. The landlords' children and I were playing in the yard and I picked up the garden hose, not realizing the landlord's son had gone and turned on the water. As it happened, the hose was pointed directly at his father.

When our landlord got drenched, he was not amused. He took the bunch of dirt-laden weeds he was holding in his hand and hurled them in my face. I can still remember how I screamed.

I can only imagine my father's fury at the way I was treated, but without saying a word, he took my mother and me inside to our two tiny rooms. No apologies were ever made by the landlord or his wife. I often wondered why my father did not confront that insensitive man who, from the very beginning, had never treated us with kindness or respect. It is only now that I understand what great courage, dignity, and humility it took to walk away from the potentially explosive situation instead of staying and telling this man what a jerk he was.

Dad, your actions that day spoke volumes about who you were. I love you, Papa, and I miss you. I wish you were here to read this.

My father passed away in December of 1994, just after I had finished my chemo and radiation therapy.

Our first real home in Canada was at 1019 23rd Street West. We found it with the help of a dear friend, Steve Penna. The Pennas were among the first Italians to make their home in Saskatoon. They ran the Red Rose Grocery Store on the corner of 22nd Street and Avenue K. Our first home was only one block from there, and I made many trips to the store to purchase candy and visit with Signora Angelina Penna. In fact, the Pennas' store became the general gathering place for all the Italian children of the community who were eager to spend their money on candy and chocolate.

The house on 23rd Street was a decrepit building that should have been torn down long before. I remember crying when my father took us to see it because I did not want to live there, but it was all we could afford. There was no way my father was going to go into debt for a house.

The dwelling was about 875 square feet. Walking in from the back door, there was a kitchen with a bedroom off to the right. Beyond the kitchen was a dining room, and to the right of that, another bedroom. From the dining room, one entered the living room which was the largest room of the house. To the right was the third bedroom, and a bathroom which my father creatively separated from view with a planter and shelving where my mother kept all her treasures.

Mom was determined to make that little house shine, and she did. Every morning she would wash the floor and clean the shabby house. The kitchen floor had an ugly brown covering of some sort, but by the time Mom got through with it, the floor shone to a high gloss.

Her embroidered doilies and tablecloths that came with her from Italy were proudly displayed.

Mom worked tirelessly to keep that house clean, but it was an effort in futility because the wood-burning furnace constantly sent a fine black soot up through the ducts. It was evident every morning when we awoke. But by noon, when I would come home from school for lunch, the place would be immaculate again and filled with the fantastic aroma of Mom's great cooking.

When my dad had saved enough money, we bought a new furnace and eventually my parents were able to renovate the house. We made it our home for many years.

At one point, my mother's brother, Pasquale, left

Pietrapertosa and came to live with us. I was very happy, finally, to have an uncle that I knew. I teased him mercilessly about his pale blue eyes, and he would explain to me: "Your grandfather Donata had blue eyes."

When my sister Rosemarie was born, I was thrilled to have a sister rather than a brother. The reason was that my father was set on naming a baby boy Rocco. I hated the name and prayed for a sister. I still remember the day she was born. Dad came home exclaiming happily that Rosamaria was "a beautiful little girl with a head full of black hair." I could hardly wait to see my sister. Later on, being the older sister, I would do far more babysitting for my sister than I would have liked!

Now there were three adults and two children living in the little house on 23rd Street.

Mom and Dad planted a lush vegetable garden, and Dad built flower boxes which Mom filled with flowers of every colour. We had wholeheartedly embraced this place called Saskatoon and made it our home.

My dad worked very hard and we lacked nothing. He even managed to save some money, despite the fact that my mother worked very little outside the home. Growing up, I recall how grateful I was that Mom was always home. During my high school years, she was always there with lunch ready when I came home at noon. I would wolf down my food, and then be on my way.

By this time, other Italian families were settling in Saskatoon. My father was always willing to lend a helping hand to newcomers and even loaned money to families for the purchase of a home. He was frequently approached for money once it became known that he loaned it interest-free. If he had the money to spare, Dad was glad to oblige.

Looking back, I see how through their example, our parents demonstrated to Rosemarie and me the necessary ingredients for a successful life.

In those days, social services were organized by a Roman Catholic nun, Sister O'Brien. On one occasion, Sister O'Brien contacted my father to help a distressed family of three who had just arrived from Yugoslavia. The husband had been killed tragically in a construction site accident just days after arriving in Saskatoon. The wife, Maria, was left with two small children, Mario and Alvera. Maria could not speak English, but because they had lived close to the Italian border in Yugoslavia, she could speak some Italian. Sister O'Brien wondered if my father could make some inquiries and find a temporary home for this little family of three.

Dad inquired around the Italian community, but it seemed everyone had the same predicament: homes that were too small. We had met Maria and her children, and our sympathy went out to them. During dinner one evening, Dad suggested that we bring the family to live with us. I don't think Sister O'Brien had any idea what a sacrifice my parents made when they took in the three of them.

Dad installed a door between the dining room and living room to give Maria and her children some privacy. The living room, the only bathroom in the house, and the third bedroom were on the other side of that door. Mom had to give up the room in which she entertained her friends. Her treasures were put away; her beautiful doilies stored. My Zio Pasquale had to give up his bedroom and sleep on a pull-out cot in the dining room which now served as our living room. Rosemarie and I were advised to make bathroom visits sparingly, and amazingly, life fell into a kind of orderly routine.

Maria and her children lived with us for one year. Today, I marvel at how smoothly my parents made life flow during that year. The fact that I do not recall those days as a time of hardship is definitely a credit to my father and mother.

And so, the house that made me cry the first time I saw it became a warm and welcoming haven in the heart of Saskatoon's Italian community.

In our Little Italy, all the children knew each other and friendships were formed effortlessly because of our common denominator--our culture. I have many wonderful memories of those days, especially the languid summer days when Mr. Lorenzo would drive his daughters Rocchina, Eleonora, Carmela, and me to Riversdale Swimming Pool for an afternoon of fun in the sun. I can still feel the wind in my hair as we rode in the back of Saverio's bright green pickup truck. At the pool we would spend any spare change we had feeding the juke box, dancing to the sounds of 'Runaway' and 'Calendar Girl'.

In 1968, we moved to a new house at 812 Avenue

L North. How proud my parents were when the four of us moved in. By then, my Uncle Pasquale had married and had a home of his own.

We kept the house on 23rd Street and rented it out.

After my father's death in 1994, the house was put up for sale. I went there to meet with the realtor, and while I waited for her to arrive, I strolled through the house. As the bright western sun spilled through the large picture windows Dad had installed, I was flooded with happy memories. I knew without a shadow of a doubt that if I had to, I could easily move back to that house and once again call it home.

In due time, my father became a Canadian citizen which automatically made my mother and me Canadian citizens. But although we were Canadian, my father raised Rosemarie and me by very strict Southern Italian traditions and standards.

I attended Bedford Road Collegiate and my four years there were fantastic. I was very much 'in the loop', even though I was not allowed to attend parties or hang out until the wee hours of the morning.

For some reason, most of the other students (except for my closest friends) seemed to think I was dating older, more sophisticated university men. Yah, right! The truth was my father would not allow me to date at all. He insisted I must stay focused on school work. I did get to attend the odd dance, musical presentation, and inter-school sports event, but that was about it. Dad and I had many tête à tête debates about his phi-losophies on life which I felt, back then, were very antiquated.

Within the Italian community it was understood that anyone interested in taking me out should be prepared to marry me. All the Italian parents thought the same way.

It did not stop the endless phone calls from members of the opposite sex. The more phone calls I received, the more determined my father was to impose a strict curfew. I had to accept that, and many were the conversations that were terminated with a polite excuse for not being able to go out on a date.

On one occasion I met Wally, a drummer in a band that was playing at a wedding. When Wally called to ask me out, I decided to be truthful and tell him about my strict Southern Italian upbringing. He retorted: "Remind your father of when he was your age" to which I replied: "That's precisely why he's as strict as he is."

We shared a good laugh and after a few more tries, Wally became resigned to the fact that I would not defy my parents and sneak out to be with him.

During the winter of 1967, my father went hunting with some of his Italian buddies. Their get-togethers afterward always brought the families together for an evening of dancing and games. On this particular occasion, the party was held at the home of Dad's friend, Steve.

Steve called my father to confirm that I was coming to the party. He said a group of young men had just arrived from Italy and he had invited them to his dinner party. He was also inviting other friends who had young daughters. Steve said he wanted to make sure there were enough young women to dance with these young men.

I went reluctantly. When the time came, I knew my parents wanted me to marry an Italian, but to this point, I had not met anyone who captured my attention. I was under no illusions that this gathering would be any different.

I must admit, though, I was curious to see these new men everyone was talking about.

The party was held in Steve's basement which was only partially finished. The staircase was fully exposed to the room in which the party was being held. One by one, we watched as the newcomers descended the stairs--first the legs, then the rest of the body.

I remember suit pants, grey-flecked-with-black, slowly descending the stairs. I watched as a handsome, dark-haired young man with a boyish grin strolled casually into the room. I knew immediately this had to be *the* Roberto all the Italian girls were abuzz about.

My heart did a flip-flop, and I learned in that moment that there is such a thing as love at first sight.

That evening, as Roberto and I danced, I remember being very upset whenever someone else would cut in. I wanted to spend the time with him and get to know him better. I already knew that, unless we had absolutely nothing in common, I was going to marry him.

Roberto was from Padova which is in the Venice (Veneto) region of Northern Italy. He had applied to both the South African and Canadian Departments of Immigration for a working visa. The Canadian Government accepted his application first, just days before the South African Government did. He, along with his lifelong friend and eventual business partner, Walter, had come to Canada just for the sheer adventure. They had every intention of returning to Italy after a year or so.

Roberto did not ask me out until August of 1969, two years later, because he knew there would be no returning to Italy if he fell in love. However, he was unable to avoid his collision with destiny, and in 1971 we were married.

In Roberto, I had found my soulmate, my lover, my best friend. I have often marvelled at the fact that if we had both stayed in Italy, we would never have met.

Walter married a few months after. He often jokes that he would still be a bachelor if Roberto had not married. Walter and Roberto have always been like brothers, and they have a friendship and a business relationship that is truly unique and enviable.

Roberto became my focus in life. He is my inspiration, and his support has always allowed me to soar on the wings of my dreams. His gentle, soft-spoken manner balances my high energy and enthusiasm for life.

After my initial breast cancer diagnosis in 1994, I remember asking if he had any regrets about marrying me. He replied: "I would do it the same all over again."

It was all of these things and more that occupied

my mind as I made my preparations for Christmas 1999. I felt full to overflowing. My cup was truly running over. I had so much to feel optimistic about and for which to be thankful.

I had endured all the chemotherapy and radiation treatments. I had even done my part by participating in a breast cancer clinical trial. Through my efforts, in conjunction with the Walk For Breast Cancer Committee, we had raised a considerable amount of money for breast cancer projects and had successfully brought the subject of breast cancer to the attention of hundreds of women, young and old, in our community.

I had done as much as any person could be expected to do for a cause, I thought. Perhaps, after seven years, it was time to give the whole issue of breast cancer a rest. It was time for someone else to pick up where I had left off. It was time to shut the door and get on with the rest of my life.

That is exactly what I determined to do, but the door refused to stay shut.

CHAPTER THREE

In January of 2001, I came to a startling realization. I had missed my annual mammogram.

Neither I, nor my oncologist, nor any one of the three family physicians I had seen in the past eighteen months had noticed the omission.

How could this happen, I wondered. I had made it a practice to book a complete medical examination just before each New Year. I was well aware that as a breast cancer survivor, it was even more important for me than for the average woman to have regular mammograms. How many women in the past seven years had I pestered about going for a yearly mammogram? Now I had forgotten my own.

Mentally, I retraced my steps.

I had gone to the same family doctor all my life, but when she retired, finding a doctor to replace her had proven to be a daunting task. Many physicians refused to take new patients and others seemed to be continually heading off to greener medical pastures.

A referral from a friend took me to Dr. A., an excellent young doctor who left no stones unturned. She knew I was a breast cancer survivor and in the first year I went to her, she sent me for an additional mammogram. I remembered clearly going for a routine check and having a clinical exam just before the New Year. That visit concluded with having another mammogram.

My daughter Cristina went to Dr. A., as well. We both trusted and respected her. Unfortunately, a year later, Dr. A. married and moved to Calgary and we had to go looking again.

We were relieved to be able to book appointments for complete check-ups with Dr. B., Dr. A's replacement.

Dr. B. was brought up to speed regarding my cancer history but apparently, it never occurred to her to check my file for the date of my last mammogram.

Cristina's appointment was right after mine. As we were leaving the office, she mentioned that Dr. B had done the clinical breast examination without having Cristina remove her bra. Hearing that did nothing to foster my confidence in Dr. B.'s competence.

We continued our search.

My sister Rosemarie mentioned a doctor from her community who had moved to Saskatoon. We made an appointment with Dr. C. who did a clinical breast exam and even asked about my last mammogram. I told her I could not recall the exact date. Fortunately, the mammogram report was in her file. "It looks fine," she said. "I do not think there is anything to be concerned about." It wasn't until much later that I realized Dr. C had failed to zero in on the exact date of that mammogram.

Cristina and I decided we would continue with Dr. C., but when I called a few weeks later to make another appointment, I was informed that she had returned to South Africa and that Dr. D. would be assuming her patients.

After having one family physician all my life, I had now seen four general practitioners in the course of 18 months. Every time I saw someone new, I had to repeat my entire medical history, along with a more immediate concern which I felt warranted an appointment with a gynecologist. I was experiencing some vaginal bleeding and wanted to have a pap smear done.

Needless to say, I was getting very frustrated. In addition to my own needs, I wanted a good doctor for Cristina who I felt required careful monitoring, given my own history of breast cancer.

While all of this was going on, my regular visit to the Cancer Clinic came up. The check-up showed everything was fine, but looking back, I realized that the oncologist did not catch the date of my last mammogram report, either. The Cancer Clinic had been booking my annual mammogram appointments in the past five years, which had made me somewhat complacent. I had become a creature of habit, feeling secure in this established medical routine.

It was late August, 2000, when I was finally able to meet with Dr. D. to discuss the vaginal bleeding. She agreed that I should see a gynecologist and made the necessary appointment. She also did a clinical breast exam, but found nothing out of the ordinary. Once again, the date of my last mammogram was passed over.

I saw the gynecologist, tests were done, and any fears I had about metastasis were laid to rest. I told Cristina I believed we had finally found a family physician to whom we could entrust our health.

By now it was January, 2001. Cristina and I had agreed to wait until the holiday season was over to book our annual medical examinations. It seemed practical for several reasons. The main one was that going for check-ups just prior to the New Year seemed to blend the years together, thus blurring the memory of when relevant tests were performed.

It was after having a complete examination at Dr. D.'s office that I began trying to pinpoint exactly when I had had my last mammogram. The only way to find out for sure was to call the Women's Imaging Centre.

"According to our records," they said, "you missed your mammogram last year. You really should book an appointment and have one done."

Naturally, I did, and I booked one for my mother at the same time.

Nearly eighteen months! It had been eighteen months since I'd had a mammogram. For a breast cancer survivor, that borders on irresponsibility. Oh well, I reassured myself, I'd had regular clinical examinations, and everything was presumed to be fine.

Soon after, I got a call from the Women's Imaging

Centre. Dr. D.'s office had faxed a requisition to them to book a mammogram appointment for me. It was something that Dr. D did routinely after every complete exam. In retrospect, it seems unfortunate to me that this is not standard practice for all doctors.

Now I had two mammograms booked. Which one would I cancel?

About this time, I began keeping a journal. I felt it was necessary not only to have a place to unload my tumultuous emotions during this unsettled time in my life, but also as a way of recording the daily events and happenings as they pertained to my medical health care and treatment. I realized I needed to take active owner-ship of my own health care.

To that end I bought a book and began detailing all the doctors visits, tests done, and the results. I pre-sented my daughter with a similar book, a lovely one with butterflies on the cover, to be her medical diary.

I blamed myself for the missed mammogram. I was learning the hard way that a person's most impor-tant and powerful medical ally is one's own self. I had always recognized how essential it is to be well-informed. I had allowed myself to be lulled into a sense of false security. I was very angry and upset with my-self for relying on the doctors and their files. How of-ten had I told women in my breast cancer presentations that they should establish partnerships with their doc-tors. Sadly, I had not kept up my end of the partner-ship.

While I was completely frustrated by my negligence, Roberto, in his calm way, pointed out the positives. He reminded me that in the past seven years, I had lived life to the max and not in fear of breast cancer.

In the end, I decided to keep the mammogram appointment that coincided with the one I had booked for my mother.

Driving to the appointment on Monday, February 19, 2001, Mom and I chatted easily about the lovely weekend we had just shared. Mom spends her weekends at our house and on Saturdays we go shopping or bake a dessert for Sunday dinner. On Sundays we go to church together, and after Mass we cook up a storm, much to the delight of Roberto, Rob, and Cristina.

At the clinic, we each had our respective mammogram. Dr. M. invited both of us into his office to look at them on the viewing screen.

I listened with some distraction as he confirmed that Mom's x-ray was just fine. I was preoccupied with my own x-ray which seemed to me to show some irregularities.

Before Dr. M. could launch into the discussion of my mammogram, I suggested that my mother go and get dressed while Dr. M. and I talked.

"May I sit down?" I asked. My legs felt oddly weak as I prepared myself for the report.

It was as I thought. Dr. M. confirmed there was need for concern. He said I should see a surgeon as soon as possible.

I made my way to the dressing room feeling numb

with shock and disbelief. It was the first time all over again.

I dressed mechanically and forced myself to focus on the immediate, which was getting my mother home. Then, I told myself, I would be able to deal with the whole idea that the breast cancer had recurred.

Before leaving the change room, I said a quick prayer asking that God would give me the grace not to break down in front of my mother.

On the way home, I tried to make conversation with Mom, but all the while my mind was repeating like a broken record: "Please God, help me...I mustn't cry...not now, not now..."

I was in a zombie-like state, but somehow I managed to get my mother home safely without disclosing my inner turmoil.

It was Monday. Roberto and the children were all at home. What would I tell them? Oh, my God, what would I tell them?

The thought of recurrence had always been hidden away in the far recesses of my mind. Well, that day was now, February 19, 2001, and the harsh realization was beginning to sink in.

I decided to make a detour to my friend Maria's house. I knew she would be home because she had Mondays off. I told her everything.

Initially, she could not grasp it. "I was shocked," she told me later. "I felt it couldn't be happening again. Surely it was a bad dream."

Maria insisted I drink a bit of Grand Marnier to settle my nerves. Both of us were crying.

"Roberto and the children have been through so much," I moaned through my tears.

"You are the one going through all this," Maria said bluntly. "Roberto and the children will be fine. Start worrying about yourself."

I told myself on the drive home that it was time to shift gears and move forward. I had been living my life backwards, blaming myself for the missed mammogram. What I needed to do now was focus on moving forward and making a stepping stone out of this stumbling block that had come into my life.

When I finally made it home, the children were busy doing laundry and discussing whose turn it was to put in the next load. I found Roberto painting the front foyer. I walked straight into his arms and told him the news. Words were unnecessary; our tear-filled eyes said it all. I told Rob and Cristina over dinner, and with conviction and assurance I added: "We have been through this before, we'll go through this again, and we *will* be fine."

Two days later, I met with Dr. G. whom I had requested for my surgeon. I liked her immediately and felt I was in good hands.

She saw two areas of concern on my mammogram. One was a starburst shape on the line of the former surgical incision; the second was a half moon shape around the nipple. A clinical exam revealed nothing. "If there is something," she said, "it is probably pre-cancerous and non-invasive."

Her diagnosis brought immense relief--followed by
a massive headache.

Once again I was in turmoil, but in the midst of it,
as my journal reveals, I received a wonderful boost of
encouragement from a most unexpected source.

Thursday, February 22, 2001

> *After a frustrating beginning to the week,
> today brought with it a pleasant and most wel-
> come surprise, a photograph of my Grand-
> mother Francesca. I have been hunting for in-
> formation, keepsakes, anything that would
> create links to the grandmother after whom I
> was named, but had never met. The 8" x 10"
> photograph could not have come at a better
> time. As I unwrapped the package, the joy I
> experienced was overwhelming. I began to
> cry, hugging the picture to me. In the photo,
> my grandmother is wearing the earrings she
> gave to my mother. Now, the exquisite red-
> gold earrings belong to me and I wear them
> often. My joy was indescribable.*

I began talking to the photograph, telling my
grandmother about the bad week I was having, and how
I wished she were here with me. I told her about all the
information I was piecing together about her, and how
she was still an admired matriarch of the family and in
the community where she had lived.

In 1999, when we went to Italy for a visit, I begged for any story anyone could tell me about Grandmother Francesca. One of my favourites was how after my grandfather Vito Rocco passed away, my grandmother stripped their bed and covered it with a dark brown bedspread to 'put the bed in mourning'. She never slept in that bed again. My grandparents were in love right to the end and their love extended to everyone who knew them.

Seeing my grandmother's photograph soothed some of the pain and hurt from my mind. It transported me, if only for a while, to another time.

The Monday after the photo arrived, I had another mammogram done at a different clinic. It confirmed the results of the first one.

A biopsy was performed and a little wire was left in my breast to mark the area of concern.

This was followed by surgery during which Dr. G. removed some of the tissue in the marked site, but left the area around the nipple intact. She was unable to detect anything visually, and excising, she said, would have meant cutting out a significant area.

The pathology report confirmed that the tissue was cancerous and invasive. The results came as a surprise to Dr. G. who had thought, because it was not palpable, the tissue was most likely pre-cancerous and non-invasive.

There was good news, however. The cancer had been detected early. That, alone, reinforced for me the fact that mammograms do save lives. My mammogram had picked up something that could not yet be felt during BSE (Breast Self Examination) or clinical exam.

I had already made the decision to have a mastectomy. The surgical removal of my left breast was scheduled for March 7. That was only five days away.

The decision had not come easily. I remember gazing into the starlit night with tears welling in my eyes. I offered my breast to the Lord, and promised Him the void would be a constant reminder of His love for me. In doing this, I was taking my despair and suffering and putting it to good use. Wasted suffering made no sense to me.

Was that moment of surrender pivotal in my life? It seems so, though I did not know it at the time.

Mentally, I began making preparations for a final good-bye to my constant companion--my left breast.

The next day, March 3, my good friend, Carmela Shearer, invited me to go to Saturday evening Mass at St. John Bosco Church. Carmela had arranged for a woman by the name of Carmen to pray over me after Mass. She had heard from a co-worker about Carmen, a visionary with the gift of healing hands.

As evening approached, I was feeling nauseous and dizzy. Roberto noticed how pale I looked and suggested I stay home, but an Inner Voice urged me to make the effort.

I took a Gravol and began getting ready.

Sitting in the pew that evening awaiting Carmela's arrival, I thought about the frigid, minus-35 degree evening three years before when I had driven to St. John

Bosco Church to do a breast cancer presentation. I recalled thinking: Why am I doing this when I could be home in front of a warm fire? On my arrival, however, I found 25 ladies eager to hear what I had to say about breast cancer. I knew instantly why I had come, and as I drove home that night, I felt very humble. Those women had attended by choice, not by appointment. They had braved the coldest night of the year to come and hear me speak about a topic that brings fear to the soul of every woman. Recalling that experience brought back fond memories. Would this night be equally significant, I wondered?

I found myself searching the congregation for this Carmen, this woman with the gift of healing hands. Would she look 'different' somehow, I wondered?

When I was introduced to her after Mass, Carmen turned out to be very normal-looking. A former nurse of French descent, she had long black hair tied in a ponytail and luminous, compassionate eyes that immediately put me at ease.

Carmen suggested I take off my coat. She said I might get very warm. I thought the suggestion rather odd at the time.

She escorted me to the altar and invited my friend Carmela and a woman named Wendy, whom I had never met before, to join us at the altar. I got the impression she thought she might need their help.

I stood before the altar, near the Tabernacle where the Hosts are kept, with Carmela and Wendy on my right and Carmen on my left.

Carmen asked me to visualize Jesus standing before me. I closed my eyes and thought of the picture
that has always adorned our home. It is a portrait of
Jesus in the Garden of Gethsemane.

Carmen began to pray, and while she was praying,
she blessed me with water from Lourdes. (Lourdes is
located in southwestern France and is primarily important for its religious history and its healing waters.)

Without knowing why, I began to sob uncontrollably. Carmen continued to pray.

When she finished and I opened my eyes, I discovered that everyone else was crying, too, including Carmen.

"Did you feel any heat while I was praying?" Carmen wanted to know.

I had not.

"I had a vision while I was praying," she told me.
"I saw the Blessed Virgin Mary with a scoop. It was
like an ice cream scoop, but smaller. More like a canta-
loupe scoop. She was scooping out the cancer, first
with a small scoop, then with a bigger scoop, like an ice
cream scoop." Calmly, yet tearfully, Carmen astounded
me by saying: "The Blessed Virgin Mary is going to
heal you."

We left the altar and walked to the back of the
church. I was in a daze, but I do remember children
running about and Carmen reminding them that this
was the House of God and that they should behave ac-
cordingly.

I did not know it then, but on that evening my

journey with breast cancer would transform into an un-relenting dance between my logical mind and my heart.

At home later that night, I was unusually quiet. I knew I would eventually tell Roberto all that had tran-spired, but at the moment, I could not. I was on emo-tional and informational overload. I was completely exhausted and needed time to rest and regroup.

The mastectomy surgery was booked for Wednes-day, March 7, 2001. Roberto had to work the evening before, but he was reassured by the fact that my close friend Giuliana would be with me. The two of us spent the evening reminiscing, laughing, and weeping to-gether.

I awoke very early that morning feeling unusually calm. There was no hysteria, no panic.

I kissed Rob and Cristina, who were still sleeping, then headed out to the car for the early morning drive to Royal University Hospital. On the way, I thanked Roberto for being the wonderful father and husband that he is. I told him that at dinner the night before, while he was at work, I had told Rob and Cristina how very proud I was of them and how much I loved them. I also assured them, albeit through tears, that everything would be fine and that I would once again turn this lemon of an experience into lemonade. "Just watch me," I said.

It was 6:30 a.m. when we registered at the hospital. Rosemarie had met us in the Admitting Department. At 9:00 a.m. a nurse came to escort us to the Operating Room. We were on the Fifth Floor; O.R. is in the basement of the hospital. Together we began the long walk to O.R. There we awaited the arrival of my surgeon, Dr. G.

Dr. G. seemed rather disturbed when she arrived. She informed us that my pre-op blood tests, which had been done two days prior, indicated my liver blood count was high. The normal range is 30 to 110; mine came out at 123. The elevation, she said, could be an indicator the cancer had metastasized to the bone or the liver, and while she remained optimistic that the invasive tissue was only in my left breast, she could not ignore the blood test results.

What she was saying was that it did not make sense to amputate my breast if the disease had spread further.

I agreed. In fact, during this whole episode, my entire being seemed to be filled with a strange and inexplicable inner calm.

Roberto and Rosemarie were sitting on my right; Dr. G. was on my left. I looked at them all calmly and stunned them by announcing: "There's nothing wrong with me. Any further test results will come back negative." I had the sense that Something or Someone did not want me to have the surgery that day.

I had a few questions for Dr. G. regarding the mastectomy.

She answered them.

I gave her a hug, and went back to my room to get dressed.

I held my hands crossed over my breasts as I walked with the nurse back to my room. Roberto and

Rosemarie followed. The nurse tried to make conversation, but no one paid any attention. I was filled with elation and wonder as the thought repeated itself in my mind: "Mother Mary has already done the surgery... Mother Mary has already done the surgery..."

When Rosemarie and I were together inside the curtained enclosure, I told her the surgery had already taken place. I said that instead of being filled with fear and turmoil, I was feeling complete peace and serenity.

Both Roberto and Rosemarie were very distressed. They did not know how to respond, but tried their best to be helpful and supportive.

Back home later that morning, the first thing I did was phone Carmen. It took three tries, but finally she answered. I told her what had happened.

"I was thinking about you this morning," Carmen said, "and a great number of people were praying for you." She had spoken with her husband about my case and his response was: "Tell this woman not to go ahead with the mastectomy until she has had another mammogram."

"I can hardly believe this," Carmen went on. "Half the city is praying for your surgery this morning and here you are at home."

She suggested I find a quiet place to sit down and she would pray for me.

I did so.

As Carmen began to pray, her voice changed. Throughout the prayer, she received visions which she would describe to me as they came, then continue in prayer. She had four visions in all. They were not visions for her, she explained; they were intended for me.

In the first, she saw the face of Mary.

The second was the hand of Jesus opening and parting a balloon.

The third, she said, was rather amusing. She saw Mother Mary, Jesus, God the Father and God the Holy Spirit playing cards and having a good time. They all seemed very joyful.

In the fourth vision, she saw Jesus saying: "I love you, Francesca...I love you, Francesca...I love you, Francesca."

As I listened, I began to sob. "I love Him, too," I said.

I thanked her for her prayer and added: "I have never played cards in my life, but anyone who knows me will tell you that one of my favourite sayings is: 'It's not the cards you are given, but how you play the ones you've got.'"

That afternoon I was called back to the hospital for a bone scan. On the way there, I asked my husband and my sister not to disturb me. I wanted to close my eyes, enjoy the warm sun on my face, relax and meditate.

I reopened my eyes as we were approaching the University Bridge that would take us across the South Saskatchewan River and up the hill to the University of Saskatchewan Campus where Royal University Hospital is located. In the park just below the Bridge is a bronze statue of a dear friend, Denny Carr, a long-time Saskatoon radio personality and humanitarian who had died of cancer not long before. Seeing the figure of Denny Carr in running gear, I joked: "I wonder if Denny was in on that card game."

At the hospital, I informed the technician that the bone scan would be a waste of time because I knew I was fine.

He gave me an injection and instructed me to drink seven cups of water and return in two hours.

I drank the water. It was a long two hours.

During that time, I tried to focus my thoughts on Carmen's visions. I had a deep sense of comfort and felt no fear. I even tried sharing some humour with my sister and Roberto, but they were both looking tired and very distraught. It wasn't surprising. Both Roberto and Rosemarie had been up since 5:00 a.m. that morning and the day was not over yet.

Nor was the roller coaster ride.

When the technician finished the bone scan, she said they wanted to do another shot of my left foot. It seemed the scan had picked up something.

Suddenly, my calm and confidence flew out the window. I felt my chest tighten with anxiety. I could sense that the technician felt she had found something significant.

"Please sit here and wait," she said as she ushered me into another waiting room. "We need to take some more pictures."

What's happening to me? I wondered. I came here today prepared to lose my breast, not my foot.

It was at that point that I fell apart. I was gripped

with the same despair that had consumed me the first time I was told I had breast cancer.

I stepped out of my dressing room and poked my head into the waiting room where Roberto and Rosemarie were sitting. I called Rosemarie to me and told her what had happened. Overcome with despair, I spoke to her in our Italian dialect:

"Oh, my poor children...what will they do without me? My poor husband..."

I realized what I was doing and forced myself to breathe deeply. Gradually, I found my centre and once again began to focus on the visions Carmen had received on my behalf. A blanket of calmness enveloped me.

"Dear Jesus," I prayed, "please help us make it through this day."

Two male technicians took some more pictures. When they had finished, they said my doctor would phone me with the results in a couple of days.

I began to sob. "I got up at 5:00 a.m. this morning and came here prepared to have a mastectomy which was cancelled," I exclaimed. I went on to explain that in January my foot had been very sore. I went for x-rays and was told there was evidence of a sprain and that the pain had nothing to do with metastatic disease.

"I have been through a grueling morning," I moaned. "I can't wait for the doctor's report."

The technicians looked at me sympathetically. They agreed with what I had been told in January, that what they saw was indeed concurrent with a sprain.

They also told me that if the disease had gone to the bone, I would be in a great deal of pain. I thanked them both for their kindness and compassion.

That evening Dr. G. called to say she had arranged a liver ultrasound for me. Once again, I was to fast after midnight and be at Royal University Hospital at 8:00 a.m. Dr. G. said she hoped to have the results of both the liver ultrasound and the bone scans the next day. (She did, and the results of both tests came back negative.)

I remember having a shower, eating something, and then succumbing to exhaustion. It was a day I would vividly remember for the rest of my life.

The only person I wanted to see that evening was Carmela Shearer. She came to our house and we lay on my bed and relived the incredible events of the past few days.

She told me about a prayer she had read. It included a line about the power of the Blood of Jesus. In my own praying, I had never given much thought before to the significance or power of Jesus' blood. This was something new to me, and for some reason, it was being highlighted for me that evening.

Finally, the day of March 7, 2001, came to an end. What a roller coaster ride it had been!

CHAPTER FOUR

The following morning, I awoke at 4:00 a.m. Roberto was sleeping soundly beside me. This was the day of my liver ultrasound. It was booked for 8:00 a.m.

As I lay in bed, it occurred to me that given the events of the previous day, and the reality that I might have metastatic breast cancer, I might be feeling panic and anxiety. Instead, I had no such emotions. I was completely at ease.

I closed my eyes, thinking I would fall back to sleep, but I could not. My mind was already too active and alert.

I lay still so as not to disturb Roberto and let my eyes wander to the beautiful antique burled walnut wardrobe that we had purchased not long before. I had found it at a florist shop where I go to buy flowers. I smiled, recalling Roberto's exclamation: "You go to Debbie's shop to buy flowers, and we end up with flowers *and* antique furniture." When I look at the lovely old wardrobe, I often wonder about the previous owners and speculate about who they might have been.

Since I was already awake, I decided to pray my rosary as I normally do each morning when I awake.

The rosary is composed of five decades, each decade consisting of praying one 'Our Father,' ten 'Hail Marys' and one 'Glory Be' plus additional prayers. The duration of each decade is about four or five minutes. Praying the entire rosary takes about thirty minutes.

As I prayed, remembering what Carmela Shearer had said the evening before, I spontaneously added the phrase to the end of each decade: *"Pour out but one drop of the Blood of Your Son Jesus upon me through the Holy Spirit and the Immaculate Heart of Mary."*

The phrase was new to me. It was not something I normally prayed. But as I repeated this phrase, something amazing began to happen. I documented it in my journal.

March 8, 2001

After the first decade, I repeated the phrase: 'Pour out but one drop of the blood of Your Son Jesus upon me through the Holy Spirit and the Immaculate Heart of Mary.' I repeated the phrase several times as though to attract, affirm and invoke the assistance of God. I needed to be explicit in my cry for help.

A strange thing began to happen. A heavy current of electricity started to enfold and en-

velop my body beginning with my toes and moving slowly upward.

My eyes were open. I was fully awake. I knew I was not dreaming. This was real, and not a figment of my imagination.

I began the second decade about five minutes later and repeated the same phrase. At the end of the second decade, no sooner had I whispered the phrase about Jesus's blood than the slow, pre-meditated, magnetic electrical surge recurred.

This time I noticed the current was deliberate and even warmer. This rolling wave of incredible energy stopped precisely under my breasts as if it were programmed to do just that.

I opened my eyes again to verify if this was actually happening.

IT WAS.

The same thing happened with the third decade. By the fourth, I was weeping as I prayed. At the end of the fourth decade, the methodical surge of electricity went up, over my breasts, paused briefly, and then travelled out through my arms and fingertips. I wanted to shout: 'Here I am, Lord. Send me, use me. I am here to do Your Will. Have mercy on me, Lord.'

By the fifth decade, about thirty minutes later, I was overwhelmed by bewilderment and

awe and a sense of, 'My God, what has just
taken place '
 Nothing happened after the fifth decade.

Tears bathed my face and I was brimming with euphoric joy and ecstasy. I wanted to wake up Roberto and tell him what had happened. I could hardly contain myself. I felt like getting up and dancing. It was as if I needed to translate this explosion of internal energy into some sort of positive action.

Intuitively, I knew beyond a shadow of a doubt that what had just taken place in those early hours of March 8 was real and it was not of this world. But what did it mean?

I could hardly wait to tell Rosemarie who was sleeping in the bedroom downstairs. I could not believe my ears when she told me that at 4:00 a.m., precisely when I had had the life-altering experience, she had also been awakened, but did not know why.

Later that morning, I put together a small package of appreciation for Carmen. I was determined to seek her out at church. I felt an unquenchable urgency to tell her what I had just experienced.

When Carmen had prayed for me at church five days earlier, I was moved emotionally but did not experience the amazing electrical heat I'd felt this morning. I knew the intense warmth was connected to some Great Power Source--*'a Power infused and shaped by love.'* It was like nothing I had ever experienced before.

The quote from Scripture came to mind: *"But if you do not say to Me: 'Go away' and you are absent-minded only because of the worries of life, then I am the Eternal Watchman, ready to come even before He is called. And if I wait for you to say a word, as I sometimes do, it is only to hear you call Me."*

That morning, every molecule, every atom, every cell of my being called out to God. Had the Eternal Watchman heard my plea?

The technician who conducted the liver ultrasound was very friendly and we struck up a conversation. Toward the end of the procedure, I asked him if he believed in Divine Intervention.

"Yes," he said without hesitation.

When the procedure was finished, he told me the ultrasound seemed normal to him, but he said the result would, of course, have to be confirmed by the doctor.

Rosemarie had come with me. We left the hospital together and went in search of Carmen.

She wasn't at church, but later, on the telephone, I told her in detail everything that had happened that morning while I was praying.

"It was the Holy Spirit healing you," she said confidently. "Do you remember the vision I had when I was praying for you of Jesus putting his hand in a balloon? Well, I need to explain that further. It was most unusual.

"Jesus entered what looked like a balloon. I know now it was a cell. He parted the cell with His hands. Then a strange thing happened. It appeared as though

Jesus did a front stroke and all of Him entered the cell."
Carmen added: "Wherever Jesus is, there is healing."

It was only the second time I had spoken to Carmen, yet it seemed as if we had known one another all our lives.

I gave her a brief synopsis of my life in the last year and explained how I felt I was at a crossroads, somehow...ready to put being an advocate for breast cancer behind me. The problem was, I said, that I did not know what was ahead for me.

"God has healed you," Carmen said without hesitation, "and He's going to use you."

"But I'm not worthy," I protested.

"You *are* worthy," she replied. "You're worthy because Jesus died on the cross for you. He shed His blood so that all people, so that you, Francesca, could be saved."

I knew that what Carmen had said about me being healed was true, but it was more than I could grasp. Oh my God, I thought, as the memories of what had happened earlier in the day resurfaced, I have been privy to something truly magnificent and wonderful. I need to be responsible with what I have experienced. What does God expect of me now?

All I could do was pray for guidance.

I went to bed early, leaving the task of answering the telephone to my family. It rang non-stop. Countless people had gone to the hospital with flowers, baskets, and cards, only to be redirected. It caused no end of confusion for all those who were concerned about my health and whereabouts.

Later, my friend Maria came over. We had a very pleasant visit. I showed her the colours of paint we had chosen for repainting our house, and we walked around with the paint samples, giggling together about this and that. Maria was astounded that I would be interested in such mundane things as paint colours. The reason was: I felt very safe and protected. Did I dare believe I had been healed? It was difficult to fully grasp the idea. Logic overruled what was in my heart.

The next day was Friday. We were gathered as a family around the table, enjoying one another's company over brunch. I told them about Carmen mentioning that her sister, Madame Hazel, said she knew me, but that I probably would not remember her. I shocked Carmen by recalling a thank you card her sister once sent me. And with that, I jumped up from the table and brought out the collection of thank you cards I had received over the years. I keep them in a huge floral box in the basement. It gave everybody a good laugh because, as they like to say at our house, if you sit still long enough, you'll get thrown out.

"We always have to retrieve the TV Guide from the recycling bin," Cristina exclaimed. "And you collect cards?" I told them it was my way of reliving special moments.

The exercise of looking through those cards reaffirmed for me the fact that I needed to keep a journal, a detailed account of this journey that I was undertaking, including a record of my thoughts and reactions.

That evening I unpacked the bag I had ready and waiting just in case the hospital called. It was as if I knew I would not be needing it anymore.

As I removed the steri-strips from my breast, I felt a deep sadness when I saw the new incision that had been made during the biopsy procedure. The lumpectomy surgery of 1994 had left my left breast abnormally stiff. The nipple turned slightly at an angle. The breast was also unusually sensitive to touch. Now this latest medical intervention had made another assault on my poor companion.

I fell to my knees and blessed myself with water from Lourdes that Carmen had given me and asked Mother Mary for continued intercession on my behalf.

My journal entry for Saturday, March 10, read like this:

> *"The phone finally stopped ringing. I drove Cristina to work, then went to my mother's for lunch. Mom still has not been told. I have been waiting for the right moment, if there is such a thing.*
>
> *We had a tranquil lunch. Sitting there watching her, I thought about how all my life I have been more her mother than her daughter. It was a case of role reversal which began when we first came to Canada from Italy and I learned the English language before she did. I love her very much and I want to protect her. Besides, I have another mother to lean on:*

Mother Mary.
I decided the news about the impending mastectomy surgery could wait for another day.

I went to church that evening hoping to see Carmen. I missed her, but she called after I got home.

"You must be loved by a lot of people," she said, and proceeded to tell me about all the people who had been praying for me. It seemed her sister had contacted mothers whose children had attended the same French Immersion elementary school as Rob and Cristina, and asked for their prayers. I was told later that four masses were celebrated in the city for me on the day of my aborted surgery. As well, the Catholic Chancery, the Catholic Board of Education, and the teachers at the Catholic schools had been faxed and asked to pray. I was completely overwhelmed and so grateful that I was lifted up in prayer by so many people.

Carmen also told me she had fasted all day Wednesday (the day of the aborted surgery) and all day the Friday before.

Fasting was something new to me. I asked her what she meant by it.

"Both those days, I had only bread and water, and I spent the time praying for you," she explained. "Fasting and prayer are very powerful."

I was astonished and grateful, and very humbled that she would do this for me, and I told her so.

"Francesca," she said, "I have done nothing. God

has healed you. It is your own faith in Him that has healed you."

That evening when Roberto came home from work, we discussed for the millionth time the events of the past few days and whether or not I should have my left breast removed.

I had had seven years since the lumpectomy surgery of 1994 to come to terms with the idea that a mastectomy could be on my horizon. The cancer had come back in exactly the same spot as before: the two o'clock position, so medically speaking, a mastectomy seemed the wisest route to take.

In a spiritual sense, I had already offered my breast to God as atonement for past sins. Jesus suffered and died for me; I was not about to waste my own suffering. I would place my suffering, desperation, and pain at the foot of His cross and plead for His mercy.

I began to ponder the very real possibility that I had been healed through Divine Intervention. Now I asked the Divine Healer and Physician to help a very special friend of mine whom earth surgeons could not help. This Special Friend was taking seven pills a day, and had been for the past five years, to stabilize a neurological condition that doctors felt could only be treated by a very risky surgery.

The mastectomy decision had been clear-cut before I met Carmen, but she had thrown a monkey wrench into my decision-making process. I knew meeting her was not a coincidence. I don't believe in coincidences. *'Coincidences are God's way of remaining anony-*

mous'.

I knew that God had led me to Carmen. It was part of a spiritual continuum that had been going on in my life since 1994, and it was now leading me toward a new awareness of God's presence.

I prayed fervently for guidance. I wanted desperately to be obedient to God's will.

"I believe I am healed," I told Roberto.

My husband did not commit himself. "I can only deal with the facts right now and nothing more," he said. "The way I see it, the tests done thus far show no spread of the disease. Therefore, having a mastectomy seems like the most logical choice. Don't you agree?"

"Before the first pathology report came in I was prepared to lose this breast," I told him, "but now I don't know if there's any need."

"You had two mammograms done at two different clinics and both confirmed the same findings," Roberto reminded me. "A surgeon opened your breast and the pathology showed invasive cancer tissue, but it was detected early and metastatic disease has been ruled out. To me, that's the miracle. All I can say is, thank You, God."

I wrote in my journal:

> *Roberto is a good man, one only has to ask any of his employees, or our children, or anyone else who knows him. This has been an extraordinary time for all of us. I am so thankful for Roberto. He is my focus in life.*

> *Memories of early morning, March 8, re-*
> *surface and sear my consciousness. I cannot*
> *fully get my head around what has happened.*
> *And so I store away the memories for*
> *later...not now. There are decisions to be*
> *made, life to be lived. I can only do ONE thing*
> *at a time.*

On the afternoon of March 11, I invited my friend Carmela Shearer to accompany me to St. Anne's Church where a Mass was being held for the anointing of the sick in the parish. The two of us had been going to this special mass for the past several years.

In church, I began to pray. Deep in prayer, I visualized my mammogram and proceeded to cut out the abnormalities--not with a gentle scoop, but with a sharp knife. Having seen the mammogram, I was able to picture the invasive tissue clearly.

When it was my turn to be anointed, Father Beck placed his hands on my head. Instantly, tears welled up that I could not suppress. *"Pour out but one drop of the blood of Your Son Jesus upon me through the Holy Spirit and the Immaculate Heart of Mary,"* I felt compelled to pray. I had never felt this compulsion before, except five days earlier when I was praying the rosary on the evening of the aborted surgery.

In the congregation were some of my seniors from the Chateau Primrose, a retirement home where I spend my Friday afternoons. As lay presider for my parish, I assist in bringing the Eucharist to the elderly.

The seniors, too, were caught up in the moment and when I went back to my seat, I saw tears in the eyes of some. After the Mass, my seniors gathered around me with hugs and kisses, asking if I had received the flowers and the card that all 32 of them had signed.

Going to Chateau Primrose every week is always a highlight for me; I receive far more than I give. The group is composed of seniors at varying levels of capability: some with strokes, some with diabetes, some using walkers, others in wheelchairs.

And then there is Maureen, one very special lady.

I met Maureen when I started my teaching career at St. Frances School in Saskatoon. Reconnecting with her at Chateau Primrose years later made me very happy. Maureen suffered a stroke which put her in a wheelchair and left her with movement in only one arm and very little speech. Although she has difficulty communicating, her vivid blue eyes always radiate a special warmth and inner glow. What a remarkable spirit she possesses.

At the Chateau, I feel like a shepherd gathering her flock. There are those who remember I am coming and greet me when I arrive; and there are those who forget and have to be called. We have it down to a science: those who remember remind those who forget.

The Communion service is followed by fellowship and goodies in the dining room. I have been going to the retirement home since 1995 and I would not trade my Friday afternoons for anything.

Monday, March 12, 2001

At the dinner table tonight, I announced that I am blessed in so many ways--the fact that so many people came together in prayer for me; the fact that I have never felt more calm and upbeat at the same time; the fact that a mastectomy is nothing compared to what could have been; the fact that I am going to write an inspirational book and call it Reflections 'NPink. *I have decided that all the proceeds from the book will go to some breast cancer initiative/research project.*

Once more I will make lemonade. Watch me. 'Praise God from whom all good things come.'

I was feeling so upbeat that I informed Roberto I was going to get our wardrobes ready to go to Mexico.

He looked stunned.

Roberto had been given an all-expense paid business trip for two to Mexico from March 21 to 25. The trip included accommodation at a five star hotel with all meals and beverages provided. With all the turmoil and uncertainty surrounding my diagnosis, the trip had been shoved into the background. Now I told Roberto I wanted to go.

"And I intend to show off my bustline while I still have it," I added.

I have always worn conservative necklines. Now it

was time to show some cleavage. The mastectomy surgery could wait until after our holiday.

Mexico, here we come!

Tuesday, March 13, 2001

> *The past two weeks have been a real life thriller for me, my family, and my friends. Two amazing events are happening, moving full steam ahead, parallel yet totally opposite to one other: a runaway medical roller coaster and a spiritual Ferris wheel spinning at full tilt. I keep asking myself: is this really happening or am I dreaming...? It seems like a drama one might see on television. Except that it was real life drama, and it was happening to me!*

The trip to Mexico could not have come at a better time. Quite literally, my brain was drained. I needed a 'time out', an opportunity to stand back and assess the amazing events of the past month.

The last of my medical tests, a CT scan, took place the day I made my announcement to Roberto. I knew they would not find anything.

Rosemarie came with me. She was very upset with me afterward because I hadn't tried to find out from the technician if the scan looked normal. I told her I didn't ask because I was not worried. (As I predicted, the test results came back negative.)

I was very, very tired, however, and needed to go home to have a shower and relax.

Rosemarie, Cristina, and I enjoyed a quiet evening together. On the way home from the hospital, we had stopped in at the restaurant to see Roberto, and decided it was easier to take dinner home than prepare it ourselves. What a great evening it turned out to be.

Thursday morning I awoke at 5:00 a.m. with a flashback from 1997, the year I decided to go and see a psychotherapist. Dr. J. was a real gentleman and I felt comfortable the instant I met him. We had a few hypnosis sessions during which Dr. J. taught me to visualize the cancer cells and mentally destroy them. At one session I told him that I wanted to purify these bad cells with holy water and heal them. No, he said, it was better to mentally destroy them.

Now as I lay there in bed, I began mentally excising any bad cells that might still be present in my body.

Dr. J. had suggested that I live my life in dynamic serenity. I had never thought of putting those two words together. At the time, they seemed paradoxical, but I had come to realize they were a powerful combination. I could continue to be busy and productive, which I was, but I could do it with serenity. Wow!

Later that day, Dr. G. my surgeon called with the preliminary results of my CT scan. It showed cysts on the right and left lobe of the liver. She said she would call again when she received a written report, and then, if there was any doubt about the cysts, a liver biopsy would need to be done.

I told Dr. G. we were going to Mexico. She thought it was a good idea and was pleased that I had chosen to do so.

Afterward, I phoned Carmen to bring her up to speed on the test results. She felt another mammogram should be done before I proceeded with a mastectomy.

I checked with Dr. M. at the Women's Imaging Centre. He said he would not recommend another mammogram, but if the surgeon or my family physician gave their approval, he would add me to the list when we returned from our holiday.

I didn't sleep very well that night. There were big decisions to be made that would affect my life forever. I was the only one who could make them, but I needed to talk to Dr. G. first.

I was not sure how much of my experience I should disclose to her. I began by asking:

"If I were to have another mammogram, what would it show now that the biopsy has been done?"

"It would show the area where the wire was placed and the biopsy was done," she said. "Not all the cancerous or suspicious tissue in that area was removed." She had not performed a biopsy of the second area of concern at all, so that would also still be evident.

"Mammograms are the best tool we have," she went on, "but there can be cancer cells that do not show up even on a mammogram. There may be no microcalcifications, yet there could still be residual disease. Your pathology report showed that cancer cells have migrated and there is some invasion."

I decided to tell Dr. G. about my experience. I explained how a woman with the gift of healing hands had prayed for me after the biopsy and that there were a number of people, including me, who now believed I had been healed. That is why I was considering having another mammogram done.

Dr. G. did not discourage me or belittle my request. She said if I wanted another mammogram, she would give me a requisition to have one done upon my return from Mexico.

She remarked that patients who are spiritual often seem to do better than those who are not. She did lay out the facts from her point of view, but she did it kindly.

There was a possibility, she said, that the compression of the breast by another mammogram might burst the recent incision. That would then require immediate surgery.

We talked more about the mastectomy.

"You realize," Dr. G. said, "there is the possibility that after the mastectomy the pathology findings may show there was no cancer found in the breast. That could be interpreted as having been cured of the disease or that the mastectomy was not necessary at all. However," she added, "the pathologist does not comb every inch of the removed breast. There could be a cell there that would escape being identified but could develop into a tumour years down the road."

The ball was back in my court. Should I have the mastectomy, or should I not?

I thought back to when I had made the decision initially. It was right after the mammogram that revealed the recurrence of breast cancer. Now I prayed that having a mastectomy was the best logical, long-term choice for my life. The past seven years had been fantastic. I wanted more of them.

Saturday, March 17, 2001

> *I realize that in life when you are given lemons, your attitude will determine whether you make lemonade or merely have sour lemons. Attitude is one of the things I can control, and how I respond to what happens around me is entirely up to me. Cancer is a personal, intimate journey. I know I could never have faced this journey without my faith and God's presence in my life. God is all around us if we only take the time to listen, if we only take the time to see.*
>
> *I will go to Mexico, knowing that three days after I get back, I will have the mastectomy. I will begin now to say farewell to my constant companion--my left breast. I take comfort in the knowledge that after I die, my body will once again be made whole in God's presence.*

As I typed with tears running down my face, I realized that the journey I began in 1994 had been one of purification. The lumpectomy surgery, followed by chemo and radiation therapy, had not fully initiated me into the sisterhood of breast cancer survivors, but the mastectomy would.

Monday, March 19, 2001

Exactly a month today, I got the news that every cancer survivor dreads: there is a recurrence. I realize this is the first time I have actually entered the word in my journal. The very sound of it instills fear--the fear of somehow losing control of my life. Thank God the fear is short-lived. Since 1994, I have learned to take fear and convert it into positive action. Action releases new-found strength which will propel me to heights never imagined.

This morning, as I lay in bed praying the rosary, I asked Mother Mary to place her mantle around me and surround me with her love. I recall that up until a few months ago, I had been praying the rosary at night, and would, invariably, fall asleep. The next morning I would be upset for not having completed the rosary. Therefore, I have decided to pray first thing in the morning when I awake, which is at 7:00 a.m.

I told this to Carmen. She reassured me that every time I don't finish my rosary, my guardian angel finishes it for me.

A lovely thought.

I felt I needed a little pick-me-up, so I made an appointment to get my hair done. I figured a new 'do' for the upcoming trip to Mexico wouldn't hurt, either.

I told Jan I wanted something different. I asked her to cut my hair with the right side shorter than the left.

While Jan worked her magic, we visited. I told her some of what had been happening since I last saw her. Jan questioned my reasoning for not going for a third mammogram when I got home from Mexico. I was finally able to put into words what I had been grappling with for days.

I explained to her how several months before, I had seen a television program about a woman in England who had the gift of healing hands. I had diligently checked the Internet for information about when this woman might be coming to North America because there is someone very special in my life whom I believed would benefit from meeting her. It had not occurred to me that I could meet a woman in my own community with the same gift.

I told Jan that I didn't need to know if my breast was healed; the decision to have a mastectomy was made shortly after the February 19 mammogram that showed the recurrence. I had already made up my mind to have my breast removed before I met Carmen. What I prayed for now was healing for my Special Friend.

On the drive home, I had a conversation out loud with God. I couldn't help chuckling. "Each day this past month," I said, "has been like a big card game. I try to play my cards the best way I know how. Now, I'm begging for mercy. If it would make any difference, I would gladly give up my breast in exchange for the healing of my Special Friend. You are the Divine Physician and Healer, God. You can do what human doctors can't."

I laughed again. "You must think me a mad woman, trying to barter with You. It must be the Italian in me!"

In the end, I said: "Your will be done. I love You."

At home, I was greeted by Cristina and my good friend Giovina. They were preparing a tea tray with goodies Giovina had picked up at the bakery. Giovina had stopped by to wish us bon voyage to Mexico.

Both Cristina and Giovina loved my new asymmetrical hair-do. I glanced at my image in the hallway mirror, and in a flash, I realized why I had asked Jan to cut the right side shorter than the left. After surgery, my left breast, my constant companion, would be gone. My hair would help me find my physical balance.

I am a true Libra at heart.

CHAPTER FIVE

Tuesday, March 20, 2001

We are all packed and ready for some fun and relaxation in sunny Mexico. Hope we haven't forgotten anything vital.

This morning when Agnes came, she asked me about the test results. (Agnes comes in every Tuesday to help me with the household chores.) *I told Agnes everything was fine, as expected. She replied: 'I am not surprised. Last week you were glowing when you told me you knew all was well. You looked empowered and very confident. You were on such a high.' I gave her a hug. She has made my life after breast cancer so much easier. I look forward to her visits.*

This will be my last journal entry before leaving.

Mexico, here we come!

The following morning, I awoke at 5:00 a.m. and began praying the rosary. "Dear Lord," I said, "please do not be upset with me for playing my trump card yesterday, but I believe life is about taking risks. It is better to risk and fail than never to try at all." With intense emotion I continued to pray: "Lord, please help me to accept my destiny with dignity and perseverance. O Lord, hear my prayer."

Even though I was determined to squeeze every ounce of enjoyment out of this vacation, the spectre of my surgery was never far from my mind. During a layover in Toronto, while waiting for our flight to Mexico, Roberto and I discussed the grieving process, and specifically, accepting and preparing for the surgery on the 28th.

Roberto assured me that his perception of me would not change after the mastectomy. He commented on my calmness in dealing with the whole issue of breast cancer again. I was so grateful for his devoted, unwavering love, and for the wonderful marriage we share.

Still, once on board the plane for Mexico, as we prepared for take-off, I could not keep my eyes from filling with tears for me and for all women who live with breast cancer. "*Gesù Cristo solo tu mi puoi aiutare*...only You can help me, Lord Jesus," I prayed silently.

We had left Saskatoon in -20°C weather. The warm temperatures when we arrived in Cancun were a lovely shock to the system.

The customs officer wished us a happy honeymoon and pleasant stay in Cancun.

"He wasn't looking at me," Roberto chuckled.

We were booked at the Fiesta Americana Resort Hotel. Our suite had a balcony that overlooked the lush landscaped hotel grounds and the breathtakingly blue Caribbean Sea. The company hosting the vacation had invited all 850 guests from Canada to a buffet dinner on the beach the first evening. From our room, we could see the round tables already spread with immaculate white linen cloths. Dozens of staff were busy preparing for what promised to be a fantastic dinner alongside the sea.

Sitting at our elaborately laid table that evening, it did not seem real. I looked up at the star-studded sky and thought: A week from today, I will be lying in the hospital after mastectomy surgery. Next week at this time, my body--as I know it--will be forever changed. Yet here I was, in this paradise, with the man I loved most in the world.

"*Carpe diem*," I told myself. Seize the day and the moment.

And I did. Roberto and I danced the night away to the sounds of the Bee Gees, the Village People, and other vintage groups. It was a night to remember. The food was delicious; the view, stupendous. We were just a few feet from the water's edge. It was a scene straight out of the movies. We were wined and dined to the max, and met some wonderful people from back home in Saskatchewan. I was so glad we had come.

March 22, 2001

Pulled back the curtains to a splendid blue sky with lots of sunshine. It felt great to be alive. The line of a song rippled through my mind: 'Oh, what a night'. I sang it as I danced around the suite, reliving the previous evening. What an incredible bombardment of the senses it had been. The diehards beach-danced on the sand until the wee hours of the morning. We, the honeymooners, retreated to our room at a respectable hour.

We spent the morning in downtown Cancun, and the afternoon on the beach. Roberto went swimming in the sea. I managed to get my feet wet.

While I was watching Roberto swim, a gentleman I later dubbed 'Halifax Harvey', tried to persuade me to come into the water and get wet. I explained that I do not fare well in the sun, that I burn and freckle and have to retreat into the shade very quickly. As we chatted, another man came by and offered me a piece of coral that he had just dug out of the sand.

When Roberto came out of the water, I introduced him to Harvey. Afterward, Roberto said: "I left you alone for a few minutes and here you were with not just one man, but two eager to make your acquaintance."

I laughed. "Give me a break," I said.

I kept the coral as a memento of Cancun.

Despite the fabulous surroundings, random episodes of the impending surgery would flash through my mind. I pictured my body without my left breast and instantly, tears would well in my eyes. Sometimes I felt I wanted to scream at the unfairness of it all.

Carpe diem, I told myself fiercely. *Carpe diem.* Seize the day.

I will, I vowed, and began to breath deeply and pray silently: "O Lord, please do not abandon me. I need Your help. Do not abandon me, Lord."

A flashback of Carmen's vision for me served as an instant sedative. It was the vision of Jesus saying: "I love you, Francesca...I love you, Francesca...I love you, Francesca." Remembering it fortified and strengthened me for the 28th.

Slowly, deliberately, I was preparing my spirit, my mind and my body, insulating myself against the surgical attack that would take place so close to my heart.

Back in our suite, we prepared for a lavish Mexican buffet dinner that would take place on the deck around the swimming pools that evening. The mood below our balcony was hurried and festive as staff transformed the poolside with round tables covered with bright pink linens, exotic flower arrangements, and balloons galore. Observing all this splendour and gaiety made me feel like a walking paradox.

The elaborate buffet featured a variety of spicy delights. A live mariachi band played beautiful music under the starlit sky: '*Guantanamera, guajira, guantanamera. Guantanamera, guajira guantanamera.*'

The soft breeze blew gently, and the sound of the rolling sea was hypnotic as I faded in and out of my private thoughts.

I lay awake long into the night and prayed that the transition to being one-breasted would be as painless as possible. *Hear me, O Lord. Please hear me.*

The next day we took a bus ride to Chichen Itza and found it a wonderful way to see the countryside.

The ancient Mayan site of Chichen Itza was as magnificent as we had expected. The Mayans laid the foundation for the Aztec empire which appeared at the beginning of the 14th century. Our guide went to great lengths to explain that the Aztecs became an empire through conquest. The Mayans, on the other hand, were not warriors, but a culture. To them, blood was symbolic of life and fertility which is why they made human sacrifices to their gods.

The main pyramid at Chinchen Itza has ninety-one steps on each side. Roberto made it to the top. I chose to remain in the shade. It was very hot and I had already climbed a steep 68 steps inside the pyramid which housed a throne and a statue of a Black Jaguar. As I watched Roberto climb this incredible structure, I couldn't help thinking how minuscule we are in the scheme of things. The fact that these pyramids were built before the wheel was invented was mind-boggling.

Thoughts of breast cancer pushed their way to the forefront of my mind on the quiet bus ride back to Cancun.

We were one day closer to the 28th. "Dear Mother

Mary," I whispered, "enfold me with your mantle. Give me inner peace, and strength."

March 24, 2001

> *Exactly seven years ago today, I had lumpectomy surgery.*
>
> *As I prayed the rosary, I wept for myself and all the women who have gone through this experience.*
>
> *For most of this holiday, I have been my carefree, happy self, and the pensive, reflective moments have been kept to a minimum. The past seven years have been fulfilling, with many accomplishments, but there were disappointments, too. With God's help, they became the springboard for vaulting me to unimaginable heights, gathering experiences, and learning valuable lessons.*
>
> *One has to live life forward, looking back only to ground or anchor oneself for future life lessons. The past seven years have been a gift that was relished to the full. I want more of them.*

We spent a glorious morning on the beach and took the opportunity to explore some of the other hotels. Later, Roberto wandered over to the tennis courts in search of a game. I swam in the pools and relaxed.

Though I was sure I hadn't been in the sun for

more than ten minutes, I ended up with a good sunburn. With a sinking heart, I realized that no matter what I wore to the farewell gala that evening, it was going to clash with my bright red skin.

Before we went downstairs, I dressed in a peach chemise that revealed a generous amount of cleavage and Roberto took some impromptu farewell breast pictures on the balcony of our suite. "We should have planned these photographs more carefully," I told my photo-snapping husband. "With this sunburn, I look like the siren on a fire truck."

But underneath the humour there was a deep sadness. "Good-bye, constant companion," I whispered. "Someday my body will be made whole again, but until we meet again, dear companion, good-bye."

No regrets. I was glad I had postponed the surgery and come to Mexico.

The gala ball was something else. It took place in the banquet hall into which Roberto and I had peeked prior to dinner. We were amazed at the sight. The tables were all covered with crisp white linen, and each chair had a swathe of floral silk fabric tied in a generous bow. Each bow was a different vivid shade: orange, green, purple, pink, yellow - every colour under the sun. The table-centres were arrangements of exquisite tropical flowers that perfumed the entire room.

We dressed formally for the dinner. My grey-blue silk and chiffon outfit contrasted sharply with the colour of my skin, but the evening went off without a hitch.

Now our vacation was over. It was time to face reality.

On the plane home, I could not keep from thinking about the surgery that would take place in three days.

Dear Lord, You died so that we might live. You suffered so that we could be saved. Please help me to accept my fate on March 28 with resolve, courage and dignity.

We arrived home in Saskatoon on Monday, March 26. My reality check came that same afternoon when I went to the office of my family doctor, Dr. D., for the pre-op tests. We had a good visit.

"I'm not the oncologist," she said, "but looking at the pathology report, there are indicators that suggest chemotherapy might be a good follow-up treatment to the mastectomy."

I was not prepared for that. Her words stuck fear in my heart.

"I am spiritual..." I began.

"So am I," she said.

I took a deep breath. "I'm prepared for mastectomy surgery, but not for more chemotherapy treatments. I believe God will look after the chemo part of it. He can direct my energy into better things than being hooked up to a chemical cocktail."

I told her that I intended to let go and let God look after that aspect of my treatment.

I pray the mastectomy will be all the treatment I need... Besides, I haven't heard from the oncologist, so I will remain optimistic. Lord, hear my prayer. Not chemo again...please God, not chemo again....

March 27, 2001

I am very hopeful and optimistic. I'm glad the surgery of March 7 was aborted because it allowed me to go to Mexico. I feel my soul has been fortified.

Tomorrow draws near. I am serene, and resigned to my fate. No looking back. Instead, I'm getting on with the rest of my life.

Went for groceries. At the supermarket, I met a lady named Emma. We have talked twice before. She told me she had just had her first mammogram, thanks to me. She thanked me for the information I had given her and she said that she was now going to have a yearly mammogram. I walked away thinking: how ironic. Tomorrow I go for a mastectomy. I believe I am walking proof that mammograms save lives.

I will continue to be an advocate for breast cancer awareness. Here I am, Lord, show me, use me to do Your Will.

Tonight I will clutch my constant companion, my left breast for the last time. I am filled with emotion. My left breast will always remain my companion, my dear companion that I will miss terribly. I will be forever left with the scar of nature gone malevolently, mali-

ciously, and malignantly wrong.

Let the tears of farewell flow as I prepare to meet the challenge head on, looking forward to the rest of my life without my left breast.

I pray: 'Almighty and most merciful Father, Creator and Preserver of Mankind, look down with pity upon my troubles. Strengthen my mind. Compose my bewilderment. Calm my inquietude, and relieve my doubts, so that if it please Thee, I may run the race that is set before me with peace, patience, constancy, and confidence.'

March 28, 2001, the day of reckoning was here.

The alarm was set for 5:30 a.m. so that we could be at the hospital by 6:30. Roberto and Rosemarie would accompany me.

I walked into the rooms of my sleeping children and kissed them good-bye, thinking sadly that once again they were being taken on a medical roller coaster ride. Cancer had become a word they learned far too soon in their lives.

The drive to the hospital was serene. We passed Denny Carr's statue, and as had become my habit, I spoke to him, much to the amusement of Roberto and Rosemarie.

At the hospital, we went through the procedure I had come to know all too well. Then we waited for the nurse who would escort us to the operating room.

On the long walk to the O.R., I tried to block out the events of March 7 when the surgery had to be aborted. *Please make my mind a clean slate,* I prayed.

Then, unlike the last time, and without warning, as we turned to head into the O.R. Waiting Room, I began to sob uncontrollably. "For all healthy women who have gone before me, and for all the women who will come after me, I will not be silenced," I vowed through my sobs. "I will not be silenced." The people in the waiting room watched quietly, sympathetically. No apologies were necessary.

Roberto and Rosemarie looked on helplessly as I struggled to regain my composure.

A nurse wrapped a warm blanket around me and walked me into the cold operating room. I lay down on a very narrow table. She stroked my hair and I fixed my gaze on her kind and reassuring blue eyes.

I began to breath deeply as four attempts were made to hook me up to the anesthetic. At that point, someone told me I could swear if I wanted to. Another person remarked: "I don't think she is the type that swears."

Oh yeah, I thought? I have my moments like everyone else...

Chaotic thoughts chased each other through my mind. Will this surgery be aborted, too? Oh God, have I made the right decision?

Dear Jesus, take pity on me. In Your pity, guide the hands of my surgeons today. I raise up my intentions on behalf of a Special Friend who cannot be helped by surgery. Lord, in Your mercy, hear my prayer. Oh, my God, I trust in you. Your will be done.

My angel/nurse continued to stroke my hair, offering ideas for visualization. I told her I was picturing Mother Mary wrapping her mantle around me. The last thing I remember was signing myself with the cross.

"I am also the Father who comforts you in all your troubles," 2 Corinthians 1:3-4.

My next cognizant action was to reach out and touch the empty spot where my dear companion once lay. The deed was done.

As I slipped in and out of consciousness, I recognized Roberto, Rosemarie, Maria, Irene, Giovina, and Giuliana. Everything else was pretty much a blur. My mother, who had now been told about the mastectomy, would come to the hospital later with Cristina.

Once again, I had my own private nurse, my sister Rosemarie, who had come to be with me.

During my stay in hospital, Rosemarie surprised me with the developed photographs from Mexico. We quickly scanned them for the ones that needed to be stored in a private place. Having been brought up in a strict Italian Catholic home, we chuckled at the thought of what Dad would have said about such photographs.

The snapshots of Mexico brought back a flood of wonderful memories, which I relived later when Rob came to visit.

March 30, 2001

> *Had a rough night with lots of nausea. Still not ready to look under the bandages. I am comfortable remembering my left breast at which I nursed both my children for a year after they were born. My constant companion served us well. I must now focus on life.*
>
> *Please, God, help me to look under the bandages. This is my Lent, my Passion, my Easter vigil. Let me be infused with a fresh love for life and move forward.*
>
> *A comforting Bible passage comes to mind: 'I will love you with an everlasting love. I shall always love you...'*

My hospital room was once again transformed into a flower shop, and the bouquets and gifts helped to dispel the melancholy of why I was there. I was ever so grateful for the many acts of kindness that were directed my way.

Rob came by to visit the next day on his way to Chemistry Lab. He happened to walk in just as the nurse was taking the drainage tube out of the incision. What fun! When she was finished, the nurse pulled back the curtain. Rob's face said it all. He looked frightened and deeply concerned. His warm brown eyes filled with tears. As he hugged me, he said: "Mom, you are one tough cookie."

I hugged him back and assured him that once

again, I would be making lemonade. "Just watch me."

April 1, 2001

> *While having breakfast, I noticed that the rail on my bed was covered top and bottom with cards that had been taped there. One was from my seniors. Two names on it had been printed with great difficulty. One was a stroke victim; the other, a diabetic. The fact that they had signed my card despite all their own problems was both a source of comfort and an inspiration. It gave me the determination to live my life forward. I realize it is a privilege to be able to take Communion to the seniors at Chateau Primrose.*
>
> *I am blessed to have so many good people in my life.*
>
> *I hope I can make it to chapel today and receive the Eucharist.*

Many visitors came that day. I was chatting with Roberto and a friend, Nancy, when Carmen walked in. I was so elated to see her. I left my company and went over to embrace her. My hospital room had a sofa against the wall, so I ushered her to the sofa to give us some privacy. Roberto continued visiting with Nancy.

Carmen wondered if the pathology report was back, and what I had done about having another mammogram before the surgery. In whispered tones, I told her the story.

Nancy, sensing I was engrossed in a confidential conversation, was kind enough to excuse herself and go.

After exchanging a few words with Carmen, Roberto also left.

Carmen and I moved to my bed and pulled the curtain around us. She showed me the rosary that she had been praying on for me since the beginning of the month. Originally, the links of the rosary were silver; now many of them were gold. The beads were blue when the rosary was purchased; now they were visibly darkening. The rosary was now a combination of silver and gold links and blue and black beads. Without question, it was going through a metamorphosis.

Carmen explained that she prays devoutly to the Madonna of Medjugorje and that rosaries changing colour is a phenomenon of Medjugorje.

Medjugorje is a village located in Croatia near Bijakovici. In Croatian, its name means 'place among the mounts.' There, in 1981, Mother Mary appeared to six children and began giving them messages. The visionaries testify that she continues to appear regularly, inviting pilgrims to peace, faith, conversion, fasting, and prayer. Mary, Queen of Peace, told the visionaries that the reason rosaries and medals change colour is to show that prayer can change human hearts, human endeavours, and human circumstance. She said, "Only peace must reign between man and God, and between men."

Carmen told me she believed this rosary changing

colour was a sign that Mother Mary was listening to our prayers. I was overwhelmed.

"May I pray for you?" she asked.

I nodded.

Carmen clasped my hands and began praying, and as she did, she had a vision of Mother Mary cradling me in her arms like a baby, her mantle swaddling me.

Carmen prayed for my Special Friend, as well. I had told her that since the decision to have a mastectomy was made before I met her, I had asked God to cure my Special Friend instead, if it was His will. Carmen asked God, in his Almighty Power, to hear my pleas and let the physical healing take place for this Special Friend of mine--if that was His will.

As Carmen prayed quietly through tears, she had another vision. She saw God the Father placing a crown of little white roses on the head of my Special Friend.

I did not want the moment to end, but by now, more visitors had arrived, so Carmen ended the prayer and once again blessed me with water from Lourdes. We embraced with a promise to see one another again very soon.

That afternoon, I had many visitors who brought get well wishes, tempting goodies to eat, and more flowers. Room 5319 literally rocked with love and laughter.

One young woman named Eva brought communion. When she arrived, she looked at my nametag and said: "I don't think there are too many Francescas in

Saskatoon. You must be the woman I have been praying for since early March."

Later that evening, when I was finally alone, the full impact of the day began to settle on me. I tried to read a book Carmen had brought for me, but I was totally exhausted--in a good way. I decided to put it away for another day.

Carmen had also given me a medal of Our Lady of Graces. I clasped it to me and began to pray the rosary. I asked God to protect Carmen and give her strength. These visions she was receiving on my behalf were surely energy-depleting. I prayed for her husband and her two young sons, as well.

April 2, 2001

> *We often get so busy with our lives that we do not stop to see and hear God in our midst. The refrain from a song has been ringing in my ears today: 'God is alive, Alleluia'.*
>
> *Dear Lord, make me worthy of Your love. Show me how I can be of service. Easter this year has a stirring dimension for me. Make me worthy.*

I finished the book that Carmen gave me. One passage, in particular, was a special blessing. It gave me the confidence to know I could look at what was beneath my bandages.

I was being discharged, and before I left, the nurse

came in and took off the dressing. Roberto had come to take me home, but it would take more than one trip to get all my gifts and belongings down to the car. We were in no hurry; we had all day.

Finally, it came time for me to take off my gown. I knew there would be no more bandages hiding my chest.

The gown dropped. I looked down and began to weep silently.

Roberto put his arms around me.

I blurted: "Jesus was crucified. He humbled Himself and became a man in order to lead us to His Father. In the blink of an eye, He could have set the record straight, yet He chose to die so that we could live."

I glanced down again and made the conscious decision that whenever I was in pain or distressed about the way I look, I would remember God's love for me and for all humanity and I would pray: 'Let me do more, and love better.'

I forced myself to take a closer look, and had to agree with everyone else who had seen the work of my earthly surgeon, that Dr. G. had done a great job.

Now homeward bound, I was tranquil and able to enjoy the drive and the glorious spring day.

Roberto helped me get into the shower. He refused to leave the bedroom until I had finished, and spent the time on the sofa, reading a magazine. Meanwhile, in the shower, I was singing loudly: "He will raise you up on eagle's wings." At one point, I paused to wonder if Roberto thought I'd lost my marbles.

Cristina helped me with my hair. When she was finished, I showed her some new dance steps I had learned in Mexico and told her about the night on the beach when all 850 Canadians were doing the actions to the song 'YMCA'. I tried to coax her to join me.

Her response was to look at me with affection and say: "Mom, you are such a dork."

I felt intoxicatingly happy to the point of feeling weak. I closed the bedroom door and lay down on my bed where I meditated, prayed, read, and dozed off. Then I began the process all over again. It was wonderful to be home.

April 11, 2001

Went to see my surgeon, Dr. G., for my two week check-up. Dr. G. began by saying she had good news or bad, depending on how I wanted to look at it. The pathology report of my left breast found there was no further evidence of cancer.

As far as she is concerned, this should be the end of the cancer.

I did not know whether to laugh or cry. Vivid memories of March 8 resurfaced. Had I had the mastectomy for nothing? My breast was gone. Nothing could ever change that.

I consoled myself with the knowledge that my decision was made long ago. By God's grace, I would now move forward the best way I knew how.

I wanted to live, to see my children graduate from college. I wanted to be there when they married. I wanted to grow old with my Roberto. I had so much to live for.

CHAPTER SIX

Wednesday, May 9, 2001

I thought I had finished my journal, but it would appear there are more entries to be made. Today I saw my oncologist for the first time since the mastectomy surgery. I had to wait for two hours before seeing her, but I felt no alarm. After all, it is now 41 days since my surgery and I feel secure in the fact that if there were any recommendations for follow-up treatment, they would already have been started.

My pathology reports would have gone to the oncologist in March.

I smiled as I recalled how Roberto and our friends were all baffled by the pathology report which found no further evidence of cancer. It was a thorough pathology consisting of 24 slides of the removed breast. It had been read by two pathologists. If the cancer Dr. G. said she left behind was still there, it would surely have been evident. Nothing was found.

At last the oncologist came into the room and we chatted for a few minutes. Then she said: "Let's get on with business."

She proceeded to tell me that I should have more chemotherapy. She recommended a more aggressive chemo regimen than what I had had the last time.

I was shocked. I assumed the mastectomy was all the treatment I needed. Worse, she said I had a little over a week to decide whether or not to have the chemo.

She explained why I had not been notified sooner. It seemed the format for reporting pathology had recently been changed. Formerly, the tumour size was listed from the *largest* to the *smallest*. Now, the reporting format had been reversed and when the oncologist glanced at my pathology report back in March, she looked at the first number. Thinking it to be the largest tumour dimension (when, in fact, it was the smallest), she breathed a sigh of relief because no further chemo was warranted. However, upon rereading the report in preparation for this visit, and noting all the measurements, she now realized the dimensions of the largest tumour were slightly over the norm. Hence, she was recommending chemotherapy.

I left the office trying to make sense of this latest development. Needless to say, I was not impressed. The pathology that prompted this recommendation for chemotherapy treatment had been sent out on March 2;

this was more than two months later.

Back home, I phoned Carmen and we rehashed the pathology reports. She asked if she could say a prayer for me. I found a comfortable spot and began to relax. When Carmen had finished, she told me of the vision she had had while praying.

She saw Jesus extending his right hand, clasping my left hand, leading me down a path with many beautiful flowers. The path was smooth and easy to walk on. Just hearing about it filled me with an inner peace and serenity.

The next day, Thursday, March 10, my sister Rosemarie came with me to see Dr. D., my family physician. We reviewed all the extensive data, both medical and spiritual. Once again, Dr. D. was extremely compassionate as she addressed each and every concern we had.

I still felt the need to investigate further. I asked if I could get a second opinion. Would she fax my records to Dr. N. in British Columbia? Dr. N. used to work in Saskatoon and was considered one of the leading oncologists in North America.

We agreed to do more investigation and confer again. Rosemarie remained adamant that I should proceed with the chemotherapy as further insurance against another recurrence. She expressed deep concern at my reluctance, however she was pleased that I had at least asked for another opinion.

That evening, I went to hear Carmen's presentation following Mass. She is an outstanding speaker and I can see why she has been given this special gift. We were the last ones to leave the church. I gave her a copy of the pathology reports on the breast that had been removed. Being a former nurse, she was glad to receive them. I introduced Carmen to my family and she blessed each one with water from Lourdes. She said she wanted to give me a blessing, too, and began sprinkling me with water. I remember teasing her that it was more like a shower than a sprinkling.

I closed my eyes and Carmen placed her hands on my shoulders and began to pray. Afterward, she hugged me and whispered: "I saw Mother Mary who told me: 'I have already showered Francesca with all my holy water.'"

I came away from church that evening with a new-found confidence that I did not need any more chemotherapy. I would not have any more chemotherapy.

Dr. D. called the next day. She had heard from Dr. N. who, after carefully reviewing my case file, recommended more chemotherapy.

I had also asked my surgeon, Dr. G., to seek a second opinion on my behalf. She faxed a copy of my report to the Edmonton Cancer Clinic, and the specialists there concurred that, as extra insurance against recurrence, I should definitely proceed with adriamycin-based chemotherapy.

After another lengthy back-and-forth discussion with Dr. D., I reiterated what I had said two months earlier, that I would let go and let God look after the chemo end of it.

The final decision was mine and mine alone to make.

I need to stress again that cancer is a very personal, intimate experience that is not the same for any two people. In 1994, I willingly accepted, and was grateful for, the medicines and chemotherapy treatments I received. Chemotherapy and radiation therapy afforded me seven more wonderful years of being cancer-free. Now, as I weighed the pros and cons, I decided that for me, at this time, I would not have further chemotherapy.

I felt very secure in the gut-wrenching decision I had made. It was based on several things: the two pathology reports, all the negative test results following the aborted surgery, and an extensive search on the Internet. In my mind, the benefits of the recommended chemotherapy treatment did not outweigh the risks. My primary reason, however, was the underlying belief and confidence that I had been healed.

Once my decision was made, Roberto, Rob, and Cristina supported me wholeheartedly.

Dear Jesus, I give thanks for access to all the medical expertise I have received thus far. Thank you for our health care system. Dear Lord, you alone know how I have struggled to make this decision.

I will let go, and let God, I wrote in my journal. *Life without risk would be dull. I will squeeze every last drop out of life. I will live my life to the full. It is in our deepest despair and sorrow that we experience the strongest spiritual growth. Divine Physician, Divine Healer, I implore You, be with me now. I must follow my heart this time.*

In Saskatchewan, May is the month for planting. As I visited the greenhouses the following Monday, Carmen's vision of me walking with Jesus among the flowers filled my mind. With my outstretched right hand mentally clasping His left hand, I enjoyed the many beautiful flowers around me. The scent of them and their vivid colours deluged my senses. I drifted happily from one greenhouse to another thinking of a refrain from a hymn: *'A banquet is prepared and my cup runneth over; my head is anointed with oil...'*

On Tuesday, I took my Special Friend to church and asked Carmen to pray over her. After Mass, Carmen led us and two women who often pray the rosary with her to the altar.

Carmen placed her hands on the head of my Special Friend and began to pray. After praying, she invited us to stay for the rosary.

My Special Friend and I remained kneeling at the altar while Carmen and the other two women went back to their seats.

We completed the rosary and Carmen added a Chaplet of Mercy for my Special Friend.

The Chaplet of Prayer has its origins in the early 1930s, when Sister Faustina Kowalska, a humble Polish nun, was given an urgent message of mercy from our Lord and His Mother to be spread throughout the world. In a vision, Jesus revealed His Loving heart as the source of mercy.

Jesus taught Faustina how to pray this special powerful prayer to God the Father, offering Our Lord's Passion in atonement for our sins:

Eternal Father, I offer you the Body and Blood, Soul and Divinity, of Your dearly beloved Son, Our Lord Jesus Christ, in atonement for our sins and those of the whole world; for the sake of His sorrowful passion, have mercy on us (or insert the name of a person being prayed for) *and on the whole world...Holy God, Holy Mighty One, Holy Immortal One, have mercy on us and on the whole world.*

When Carmen was finished praying, she came to talk to us. She asked my Special Friend if she had experienced any heat.

"Yes," she replied. "I felt very, very hot. I'm sweating right now."

Heat, Carmen told her, was a sign of healing. She asked us to note that the church was very cool, and indeed it was. I was wearing a warm wool blazer.

Carmen went on to say that she had felt the heat the moment she placed her hands on my Friend's head at the altar, but the heat she experienced while praying the Chaplet from the pew was even more intense.

My Friend, who was looking fatigued and teary-eyed by this time, told how every time her name was mentioned in the Chaplet, she had felt very, very hot. "It felt like a 30 degrees plus kind of day," she said, "but even warmer."

Carmen said she believed a healing had taken place. Whether it was for my Special Friend or for one of her family members, she did not know. All she was certain of was that a spiritual, emotional, or physical healing of some kind had taken place.

She also described the vision she had had while praying. It was the same vision she received when I first spoke to her about my Special Friend: she saw God the Father, with Mother Mary near, placing a crown of little white roses on my Friend's head.

Friday, May 18, 2001

Walked to church and spoke candidly to Karen, who works in pastoral services at St. Anne's Church, about the events of the past few months. The doctors here, along with a second and third medical opinion, now concur that because there was no metastasis at this time, having systemic treatment would provide further insurance against recurrence and get rid of the problem once and for all. The chemotherapy they are recommending is nick-named 'The Red Devil.' The therapy would take place once every three weeks for six months.

I have been on a marathon of exhaustive research and collaboration. My head is swimming with information.

There is no Mass on Fridays, so we prayed in the Chapel. After prayers, I outlined my course of treatment to Karen.

My mind is made up. I told her that instead of going for chemotherapy once every three weeks for six months, I would go for prayer therapy treatment. I would ask Carmen to pray with me, over me, and for me, and let the Big Boss worry about any little cells that might have escaped into my bloodstream.

On the way home, I decided that I would fast for the day, eating only bread and drinking water. I had been open to the idea of fasting for some time, but didn't know when to start. I was reminded of Good Friday, when Jesus died so that we could have life. "Let the fasting remind me of His great love for each of us," I prayed, "and let it be a small offering as a token of my appreciation."

I recalled reading once that fasting allows an individual to become a channel through which God may work. It purifies the mind that is in a condition of mental confusion. Well, that certainly described how I had been feeling since my visit to the oncologist nine days ago.

I was amazed how energized I felt when I awoke the next day. The fasting made me feel great, so I went for an early morning walk to a point on a scenic ridge above the South Saskatchewan River.

There I met an elderly gentleman by the name of Walter. No sooner did I sit down on a bench than he began to tell me that his father never loved him.

What is it about me that makes people want to tell me their life story, I wondered?

Walter went on to tell me that his mother died in the Sanitorium, his son was a policeman, and he was a rehabilitated alcoholic. He told me that he now worked with Alcoholics Anonymous and was an exemplary member of the community. He had been given 'Citizen of the Year' and countless other awards, and all the while no one knew of his private battle with alcohol.

Walter asked what I did for a living. I told him I was a homemaker and a former teacher. He observed that teaching was one of the most important professions.

I listened as he rambled on, but at one point, I felt pressed to interrupt. "Just a minute," I said. "What do you mean, nobody loves you. God loves you. He has always loved you."

Walter nodded sadly. "I realize that now, but I didn't as a child. I know there is a Great Force out there. I work with teens who are addicted to drugs and I have seen some pretty amazing turnarounds."

My encounter with Walter left a strong imprint on my heart. I realized there were many, many children who grow up without love. My own father never said the words: 'I love you,' but he showed me all the time that he did.

As I walked back home, I prayed for all the Walters of the world who grow up without love.

I also prayed for my own dilemma. I needed confirmation and assurance that I was doing the right thing in choosing prayer therapy over chemotherapy. It came in a rather unusual way.

On Monday morning, my mother called at an unusually early hour. "Why are you calling?" I asked. "Everyone is still sleeping."

"I have something very urgent to share with you," Mom said. "This morning I had a dream. It was so intense, I was awakened. In the dream, I saw your father standing in the bedroom. He called out to me: 'Meluccia, Meluccia!' Then Mom began to give a very detailed description of what he was wearing. "Your father said, with urgency in his voice: 'Francesca is okay. Francesca is okay.' Then he disappeared."

When I was diagnosed with breast cancer, we weren't sure how much, if any, my father understood about what was going on. One day, Mom recounts, she went to my father who was sitting in his LazyBoy chair and said: "Vincenzo, Francesca has breast cancer. Do you understand? Pray for Francesca. Vincenzo, pray for our daughter." A tear rolled down my father's face and Mom knew that, yes, he had understood.

My father died of Alzheimer's in December of 1994. Following his death, our family experienced his presence on several occasions.

The morning of his funeral, my mother and Rosemarie were preparing to go to the church when the entire house was filled with a scent they could not account for. The next day when my sister and I were going to the bank for our mother, the car was filled with the same unusual scent. I opened the window, but it wasn't coming from outside; we ruled out mechanical problems. Then, suddenly, I began to cry.

"It's Dad," I said, "letting us know that he is fine where he is. What we're smelling is the scent of incense that they use at church for funerals. That's what it is, Rosemarie."

The episode with the incense happened a few more times. One evening, my mother was going up the circular staircase in my home to the second floor. The staircase is in a large foyer that is open to both the main and second floors.

Suddenly, I heard my mother call: "Francesca, come quickly."

I rushed to the foyer to find the whole space filled with the scent of incense. My mother said it had followed her up the stairs.

Cristina was quite upset that Grandpa hadn't waited to reveal his presence until she was around, but her turn came two months later on a very cold winter morning as I was driving her to school.

"Yuk," she exclaimed suddenly. "What's that smell?"

Once again, the car was filled with the scent of incense, this time, very profusely.

I laughed. "Cristina honey, that's your Grandpa

letting us and you, in particular, know that he is with us." I have since learned that the smell of incense is symbolic of the presence of Jesus.

Now, when I repeated my mother's story to Cristina, she said: "Well, Mom, how many more signs do you need?"

Thursday, May 24, 2001

> *Yesterday I tried to call the Cancer Clinic to inform them of my decision not to have further chemotherapy treatment, but after playing telephone tag for most of the morning, I gave up. I knew I would be going to Royal University Hospital today, and could slip over to the clinic when I was done.*
>
> *While visiting with Nancy at the clinic, my oncology nurse, Charlene, came in.*
>
> *I thanked them both for everything the great staff at the Clinic had done for me, and reassured them of my continued support for the Clinic now and in the future. Then I proceeded to tell Charlene that I had decided to forego the chemotherapy because, in my heart, I knew no further medical intervention was necessary. I said I intended to let go, and let God take care of me.*

Nancy and Charlene assured me that the Clinic would always be there for me if I needed their help. I left, feeling at peace.

My plan of action would encompass my spirit, my body, and my mind. The spiritual part was progressing, and I had taken care of the body part by having the mastectomy. I was also channelling my physical energy into redesigning my garden and creating a special place for a statue of Mother Mary.

Now, I had to proceed with the mental part, the mind.

Years before, when Roberto and I were engaged, we went to see Reveen, a well-known hypnotist and showman. During the show, Reveen challenged the entire audience to a hypnosis exercise. It was a test of the power of the mind, he said.

He explained that only persons who wished to should participate and added that only those who were very focused and open to his suggestions could be hypnotized. He cautioned that those who became hypnotized would have to come on stage to be released from the hypnosis. I recall thinking that I would try it, but I did not believe it would work.

The lights in the auditorium went down. Reveen asked us to close our eyes, lock our hands together, and focus exclusively on his train of thought.

I was aware when the lights came back on. I could also sense that Roberto and the people around us were no longer participating. I kept my eyes shut and followed Reveen's suggestions.

When it was over, Reveen asked those of us who still had our eyes closed to open them. He then instructed us to try to pull our hands apart. If they did not come apart easily, he said, we should proceed to the stage area and he would release them.

I opened my eyes, but I could not pull my hands apart.

Roberto was amused. So were the people around me, but I was scared. I told Roberto I wasn't kidding. I could not get my hands apart.

At that point, he tried to unlock them, but he couldn't. I didn't want to go on stage, so Roberto tried harder. It took incredible force using both his hands before he could pry mine apart.

The people around us were intrigued and amazed, but Roberto was clearly shaken. It was as though my hands were cemented together. The experience left us both baffled.

Little did I know that many years later, this experience in focus and concentration would play a valuable role in my battle against cancer.

I began to use the techniques I had used since 1994 when I was first diagnosed with breast cancer. Happy, my Inner Guide, became my ally once again.

I began the meditation and visualization process. The format was the same, but something had changed. As Happy and I walked through the autumn woods, instead of turning right to a house, we turned left to a chapel. I could not visualize the outside of the chapel, but the inside was very distinct.

The interior is simple--white plaster walls and arched stained glass windows on both sides of the chapel, with a free standing crucifix in front of the altar. There at the crucifix, I would bind myself to the foot of the cross and ask for God's mercy. Then I would sit down close to the crucifix and Happy would hook me up to an IV filled with holy water. The holy water was the systemic treatment for which I had opted. It would act like acid on any renegade cells, fizzing and disintegrating them, never to return. Happy was always there with his hand on my left shoulder as I prayed the rosary.

Tuesday May 29, 2001

Prayer Therapy Treatment #1.

Went to church. After Mass, stayed behind with Carmen and four other people to pray the rosary. While praying, I began my visualization process. Around the fourth decade, I began to sob.

Happy, my Inner Guide, who has been a white Easter bunny wearing a bright blue vest, takes off his head. For the first time I realize that there has always been someone underneath the costume. Now I discover that Jesus is under the costume. Jesus has been my Inner Guide all along.

While praying the rosary yesterday, I could sense in my visualization that Happy was trying to change or transform. I opened my eyes to prevent it happening. After all,

Happy the bunny has been my Inner Voice and my guide in times of trouble for the past seven years. I was reluctant to allow my mind to change direction.

Today in church, I realized there is no change to be made because Jesus was under the costume right from the start. I had simply allowed my mind to be obedient to what I was seeing. The past seven years have led me to where I am today. I feel so humbled.

The systemic imagery treatment was non-intrusive and peaceful. I had a sense of contentment and peace that was beyond description.

Friday, June 1, 2001

After a three month absence, I returned to Chateau Primrose to do the Communion Service for the elderly. I have never felt more appreciated. The seniors are delighted to have me back.

I thanked everyone for their prayers and the flowers.

Together, we celebrated the Eucharist.

Cristina came along and did the Prayer Petitions. The seniors are all so happy to have her come.

About that time, preparations were being made to

celebrate Roberto's and my 30th wedding anniversary at the lake with my sister and her family. We had a wonderful time together.

Monday, June 4, 2001

>*Went to church. After Mass, five of us prayed the rosary with Carmen. She gave me a very special gift, the rosary that had changed colour while she was praying for me. This was the rosary whose silver links had turned to gold, and whose beads had gone from pale blue to black. She asked me to take it. She said it was meant for me, and today confirmed it.*

After the rosary was completed, Carmen explained that when we were praying the Sorrowful Mysteries, during the second mystery, she had a vision. She was obviously shaken. With tears streaming down her face, she told me about it.

"I saw Mary tending Jesus' wounds with your breast tissue as the soldiers flogged him and ripped open his skin. I noticed that the tissue was whitish-grey, and that it went into the wound like thick salve. Mary was smoothing it in, and I could feel the relief in Jesus as this was happening. It was like your breast tissue was easing his burden."

She looked deep into my eyes. "Francesca, all of what you are going through is your purification. It is taking place slowly, thank God. He is going to use you after you are purified and as you are becoming so. Your story is a faith builder and God knows just how to use it to bring people to Him.

"Do not concern yourself about how this will all come about," she told me. "God will guide you gently through it all. Doors will open, and it will be apparent that you must walk through them. You will find yourself in unusual situations, situations that only the Holy Spirit could arrange. Go with the flow, because you are being led by God Himself. Trust him. He will not let you down."

How do you respond to a pronouncement like that? All I could do was offer myself completely to God to be used as He chose.

Wednesday, June 6, 2001

While praying and meditating, I find myself in the chapel in the autumn woods. But not only am I in the chapel, many of my friends were there, as well, all lined up to receive a blessing from Jesus. I was surprised because my meditations have always consisted of just me and my Inner Guide.

After everyone left, I was alone with Jesus who accompanied me to the exit stairs. I climbed the ten stairs to the top. At the top, I turned around and looked down. Jesus transformed into a dove and flew away.

Slowly, I came out of my meditation, feeling very happy and content.

Sunday, June 10, 2001

Woke up at 8:30 a.m. and began to pray the rosary. Most often when I pray the rosary, I focus on one of the mysteries in the life of Jesus--Joyful, Luminous, Sorrowful, or Glorious. In times of greater need, I seek my Inner Guide and the format is always consistent. On rare occasions, I receive unique, vivid imagery.

The procedure is always the same. I begin with breathing exercises, followed by finding my Inner Guide. Once I am mentally where I want to be, I commence saying the rosary.

Today, my Inner Guide took me through the forest to the chapel. Inside, the routine was the same. I kneel down in front of the freestanding crucifix and ask God to have mercy on me. Then I sit down and Jesus comes from behind the crucifix and hooks me up to the systemic treatment of holy water.

Today, I noticed that the IV bottle had a red solution in it instead of white. As I continued to pray, I realized the solution is Jesus' blood. I was not alarmed because I remembered that blood is a sign of fertility and life, a sign of Jesus's immense love for each of us.

I continued to pray.

While I was sitting, I saw Mother Mary place a mantle around me. Then I found myself standing with Mother Mary, under her mantle. Mother Mary was holding an adult Cristina as one would hold or cradle a baby. She took Cristina to Jesus who was kneeling in prayer. Jesus placed his hands on Cristina's head. Then Mother Mary picked up Cristina, who had now been transformed into a baby, and swung her high into the air in front of the crucifix. As she held her, a drop of blood rolled off the crucifix and onto Cristina's head.

Near the end of the rosary, when my systemic treatment was over, Mother Mary handed Cristina, as a baby, to Jesus. Jesus sat Cristina on his left arm, as one does a little child, extended his right hand to me, and led us both to the exit/entrance. When we reached it, He stood Cristina on the ground and she became an adult once more. We both hugged Jesus and began our ascent to the top.

When I had finished praying the rosary and the Chaplet of Mercy, I opened my eyes. All I could say was: "Wow!"

I told the story to Cristina. She smiled. "That's so, so beautiful," she said. "Did you tell Dad and Grandma?"

I was not sure what to make of it all, but I knew I wasn't afraid. I felt very, very safe, and full of joy at the realization that God had become a personal, integral part of our daily lives.

CHAPTER SEVEN

Tuesday, June 12, 2001

Something strange has started to happen. I have noticed that since I began praying the Chaplet of Mercy, I have been receiving interference whenever I begin my rosary. Three times today, a strange force sabotaged my praying the rosary.

It is too late to catch the nine o'clock Mass at St. Mary's Church, but I will go to noon Mass at St. Paul's. I feel this urgency to get myself to church.

I set out early for church to make a fourth attempt at praying the rosary. I parked my car, then realizing that the meter behind me had over an hour's worth of parking, I decided to back up to that spot. When I went to restart the engine, the key would not turn in the ignition. After four or five tries, the car finally started, but by this time, someone else had taken the parking spot.

I was ticked, but I knew that in order to pray the rosary and meditate before Mass, I needed to go into church in a tranquil frame of mind. I did some deep breathing, made light of what had just happened, plugged the meter, and went inside. To my great relief, I was able to pray the rosary and begin my meditation and prayer.

Afterward, I acknowledged what I had not wanted to face earlier. I fervently believed in God, and I knew there was a force out there opposite to God, but I did not like to even give it a name. I confronted it as I drove back home, speaking aloud, as I often do when I'm alone in my car.

"I am very, very strong willed," I declared, "and I will not be defocused. So go fly a kite and leave me alone!"

Satan's biggest triumph is getting people to believe he does not exist - Father Slavko.

When I got home, I noticed that Carmen had been trying to call me. I phoned and relayed my concerns.

"Am I out of it?" I wondered aloud.

"On the contrary," she replied. "You are very much with it."

Carmen said she would pray for my protection and suggested that every day when I wake up, the first thing I should do is ask God to protect me from all spiritual and physical dangers.

At the end of our conversation, Carmen invited me to a prayer cenacle (a group of people who come together to pray the rosary) which takes place at her home every Tuesday. I agreed to go, and said I would invite Cristina to come, as well.

Wednesday, June 13, 2001

> *The cenacle was a wonderful experience for both Cristina and me. Thirty-one people were there. I was inspired by the reverence and fervency with which everyone prayed, and was pleasantly surprised to see so many young people in attendance. That filled me with hope.*
>
> *Cristina and I both agreed the prayer cenacle at Carmen's house should become a regular part of our lives.*

Carmen called later in the week to ask if I would go with her to the hospital on Saturday to pray for a man named Marc. He had been my children's teacher and was one of the best teachers they ever had. Marc was very ill and had agreed to have Carmen and me visit.

I had to leave a wedding service early to get to the hospital on time. I was not sure what to expect; I had not seen Marc since he taught my children ten or so years earlier. The moment I entered the room, I instantly felt at ease and was glad I had come.

Carmen told Marc a little about herself and said she would like to pray over him. She asked me to place my hands on him while she was praying. I was standing at the foot of his bed and placed my hands lightly on top of the sheets and blankets covering his feet.

Throughout the prayer, I experienced very deep emotion, and felt an intense power surge go through my body.

After the prayer, Marc said: "I feel as if something has been lifted out of me."

"Did you experience any heat?" Carmen wanted to know.

Marc had not, but he did feel somewhat light-headed, he said.

Both Carmen and I left our telephone numbers with Marc and promised we would continue to pray for him.

Thursday, June 21, 2001

Prayer Therapy Treatment #2
Today would have been my second che-motherapy treatment. I went to church in-stead. After Mass, five of us prayed the ro-sary. Carmen then ushered Louisa, Jeanette, and me to the altar. I knelt down. Carmen, Louisa and Jeanette placed their hands on my shoulders and Carmen began to pray.

She had a vision in which she saw me kneeling at the foot of a crucifix. Drops of blood were falling off Jesus's body and being absorbed into my skin. Carmen prayed for my restoration to health.

She told me afterward she had discussed the vision of my left breast tissue being used to ease Jesus's pain with her spiritual advisor who said it was very similar to the imagery in Isaiah 53, and suggested I read the chapter for myself.

Louisa, a lady I would love to adopt for my grandmother, told me how precious I was. I thanked the women for their prayers. We hugged and parted.

I left the church feeling very much in tune with my inner self. I am grateful for the prayers, and I thank God for bringing these people into my life.

Sunday, July 1, 2001

Roberto's niece, Elisa, from Padova, Italy, arrived today from Sacramento, California, where she has been working in laboratories for the last five months. Elisa is working on a PhD in molecular biology. We are all pleased she came to Saskatoon before going back home.

In the evening, Elisa and I were left alone and I brought her up to speed on what has been happening to me in the past few months. Her eyes kept filling with tears as she listened.

I was curious to hear her response. She is, after all, a scientist.

She said: "Zia (aunt), you talk about Jesus like He is your amico (friend)".

Elisa went on to say that it was obvious to her why this was happening to me. "*You* mobilized an entire city in support of breast cancer. Think what you can do now.

"Do not question, Zia. Accept it for what it is. Your serenity and peace are apparent. Most people would be frightened and confused."

Tuesday, July 3, 2001

Pray Therapy Treatment #3
    Elisa went with Christina and me to the prayer cenacle at Carmen's house. The gathering was much smaller than usual. Only about 19 women were present. Most of them were familiar with my story and had been praying for me since late February.
    Carmen started out by asking the Lord to protect me and to hide me in His wounds. She continued with the prayer, and when she was finished, she began to cry.
    Carmen shared with the group the vision she had had previously of Mother Mary using my breast tissue as a salve for Jesus's wounds.

"This evening, as I was praying for you," she told me, "I saw Jesus with open wounds. In those wounds, there was a greyish substance. It was your breast tissue".

"The Holy Spirit will show you what He wants you to do," she went on. "It will be your choice whether you want to be an obedient servant.

"It is useless to try and figure out such things, or to find answers to all your questions. Just go with the flow. You will know what to do because the Holy Spirit will be using you as a tool for His work."

Tuesday July 24, 2001

Prayer Therapy Treatment #4
This would have been my fourth week of chemotherapy. As agreed, Carmen prayed over me.

While she prayed today, she had two visions. In the first, she saw Mother Mary showing me many veils. Moving the veils aside one by one, Mother Mary showed me what was behind each one.

She also saw many rose petals.

The second vision was of me sitting in a chair with a teacup in my lap. The Holy Spirit was pouring tea for me. The cup was overflowing. Tea went into the saucer and onto my lap, and all the while, the Holy Spirit kept on pouring. Carmen said the Holy Spirit was going to use me for His work here on earth.

By this time, waves of heat were washing over me and I was weeping quietly.

The next day, while I prayed the rosary, I remembered Carmen's words: "You will know what to do when the time comes. It is like having a built-in red light or green light. You will know. Just trust Him."

My first green light came much earlier than I expected. Later that same day, while I was visiting my mother in the afternoon, my sister Rosemarie called from the lake where she was staying at the family cabin, and asked to speak to me.

She explained that a friend of hers, Jean, was going through a crisis situation. "Would you please pray for Jean and her family?" Rosemarie inquired.

How odd, I thought. My sister had been somewhat skeptical about all the events that were taking place in my life. Now here she was hunting me down to ask for prayer.

Before I could respond, Rosemarie put Jean on the phone.

I listened politely as Jean gave a brief synopsis of what had been happening. The conversation ended with me telling her I would pray for her and her family. We agreed to keep in touch.

My sister said thank you and signed off.

Mom and I often pray together in the afternoon, so I suggested we pray for Jean and seek guidance for her.

I began to pray the Chaplet of Mercy. Carmen had said the Holy Spirit would be my guide, and that what I needed to do was have faith and trust in Jesus. At the moment, praying the Chaplet of Mercy seemed the right thing to do.

I was not at all prepared for the tremendous heat that began to move over my body. It was the same heat I had experienced on previous occasions. Now it enveloped my entire being.

I continued to pray the Chaplet.

When we had finished praying, Mother dialed Rosemarie's number. I grabbed the phone and said:

"Rosemarie, put Jean on."

I explained to Jean about the special prayer, the Chaplet of Mercy. We discussed the fact that she is Lutheran, not Catholic, and was therefore unfamiliar with the rosary.

"But I am a Christian," she said, "and I often pray in the form of talking to God."

I told her it did not matter what religion she was. If we believe in Jesus, we are all headed down the same road. We are all God's children.

"What will happen?" Jean asked.

I told her that, together, we could ask for God's mercy and intervention in her life and her family's. "The choice is yours to make," I said.

Jean said she would like to have me pray.

This is something totally new for me and I was caught off guard. I thought back to the first time Carmen had prayed for me, and suggested that Jean find a quiet corner. I asked her to visualize Jesus. When she was ready, I began to pray.

As I prayed and used her name in the prayer, I began to feel the now-familiar heat. So did Jean. I had just barely gotten started when Jean exclaimed: "I don't know what's happening, but something is happening. I feel fuzzy and very warm all over."

I told her I felt the same way.

I continued to pray.

Jean interrupted: "What's going on? I have never felt like this before."

I asked her to refrain from commenting because the interruptions were making me lose my focus.

When the prayer was over, Jean thanked me. "I'm not sure what happened," she said, "but I feel at peace."

No words could describe how I was feeling. To say I was perplexed by what had just taken place is an understatement. On the way home that afternoon, I stopped at the cemetery to visit my father's grave. I asked him to watch over me and to pray for me.

What a totally incredible, unexpected experience it had been. I was astounded, fascinated, and mesmerized by the power of prayer.

Prayer is a necessity, not an option, for daily maintenance.

Some months later, Jean wrote me a note describing the experience from her perspective:

> *"Francesca, when I spoke to you on the phone from Rose's cabin, your gentle and kind voice gave me a very warm feeling. I knew all the wrong would become right. I knew I was going to feel better. As we spoke and you prayed to Jesus to have mercy on our souls, I felt like the weight of the world was being*

lifted from my shoulders.

That day, you and I envisioned Jesus and recited the Lord's Prayer together. During that time, I experienced a feeling that I have never felt before in my life. While standing, I experienced an inner heat that passed through my body like a current of electricity travelling in slow motion. From the soles of my feet, this heat travelled upwards throughout my entire body. At the time, I was left with a feeling of calm and inner peace, and to this day, when life gets hectic and stressful, I think back to the day we spoke, and that calm, peaceful feeling returns. Often, over the past two months, the exact vision of Jesus I had that day will come to me."

My response to Jean was this: we all have equal access to God. It does not matter who we are or what position we hold in life; God waits patiently to be invited into our lives. On that particular day, Jean, through me, extended an invitation to God to intervene in her life and He did.

God and only God can heal. We are mere instruments in allowing ourselves to be used for whatever it is that He wills.

Tuesday, August 14, 2001

Prayer Therapy Treatment #5
After the cenacle was over, eight women remained. We sat in a circle. Carmen informed the others that I was having Prayer Therapy #5, and gave a brief summary of my story.

With her hand on my shoulder, Carmen began to pray. As she was praying, she had another vision. This time she saw Mother Mary enter the circle. A bright light emanated from her.

Mother Mary touched me and I became enveloped in the light. She then took my left hand and led me down a path.

On the way home, a fond recollection came to mind of an incident that had taken place more than a year before. For a period of a few weeks, my right wrist was always very sore when I awoke in the morning. I could not think of anything I had done that would make it sore, and being a cancer patient, I was thinking I should go and see the doctor.

Before going to sleep one night, I prayed specifically for help and wisdom in regard to my hand. The next morning, as I was getting out of bed, it was as though a voice said to me clearly: "You fall asleep clutching the rosary. Those muscles in your right hand have been working all night long."

Of course, I thought with a smile and happily informed my husband: "My sore wrist is due to rosary tendonitis." Since then, I have made a conscious effort to place my rosary under my pillow or in the pocket of my nightgown.

Tuesday, September 4, 2001

Prayer Therapy Treatment #6
Today would have been my final treatment with chemotherapy. I was unsure whether to have prayer therapy at church or at the cenacle. There were twenty-four people at the cenacle. It was a wonderful evening of prayer.

At the end, Carmen asked if I wanted my last prayer session that evening. I told her I wasn't sure and asked what days she would be at church that week. It turned out that only six women remained for additional prayer, so I opted to stay.

We all sat in a circle. Carmen was on my left and placed her left hand on my shoulder. Marie Clare placed her right hand on my shoulder. Everyone else joined hands. No sooner had Carmen begun to pray than I felt the intense heat. It was as though I was being plugged into an electrical generator.

I knew intuitively that I was safe, and that this was a good thing. Unspeakable joy washed over me.

With eyes closed, I acknowledged aloud the tremendous heat I was feeling.

Suddenly, Carmen began to weep.

"Mother Mary is present," she told me. "I see her giving you a hug. She's saying: 'I love you, my child.' Mother Mary is giving you a bouquet of white roses."

"What an overwhelming experience of God's presence this has been," Carmen remarked as we all prepared to go home.

This is the end of my prayer therapy, Lord. I don't know what the future holds, but whatever it is, I will never stop trusting You.

CHAPTER EIGHT

Saturday, September 8, 2001

The summer has been fantastic. My family from Italy was here for four weeks. Many memories of sunny, laughter-filled days linger. But when all the company left on August 23, there seemed to be a nostalgic melancholy in our home. I have found it increasingly difficult to get back into a routine.

This morning I made myself resume the 5 km walk that was part of my routine. Reluctantly, I prepared to go out. It is a great day for a walk, and it is also the feast of the birth of Mary. Happy Birthday, dear Mother.

Connie, a good friend, gave me a digital rosary. I put it on my finger and began to pray for my family as I walked.

What a glorious day. Why did it take me so long, two weeks, to get back into the swing of things?

My friends have been hounding me about when I am going to end my journal. They are anxious to read what I have written. They have been given bits and pieces since early March and are becoming impatient. I keep telling them that I will know when to wrap up my documenting.

Well, today is that day. This will be the end of my journal. What a perfect day...the birthday of Mary.

Arriving home after my walk, I phoned Cristina at work to invite her to go with me to Mary's Birthday Mass at 5:30 p.m. and to go out to dinner afterward. It was a day to celebrate.

On a physical level, it seemed that my breast cancer journey had reached an uneventful plateau and there was nothing more to document. But some invisible umbilical cord kept drawing me back to my journal.

Wednesday , October 4, 2001

Went to visit Irene in the hospital. Sadly, my long-time friend has become another breast cancer statistic.

While making inquiries about her in Recovery, I was pleasantly surprised to see the nurse whose face is still etched in my mind. Seeing her transported me back to March, 1994, when I awoke after lumpectomy surgery and saw the face of one of the kindest human beings you could ever want to meet: this nurse.

I remember the day like it was yesterday. I had just awakened from the anesthetic and the surgeon told me it was breast cancer, and that he had taken out the suspicious area, but left my breast intact. I recall telling the nurse that I had two young children who still needed their mother. I began to cry. This woman, who had been comforting me by wiping my face and stroking my hair, listened with genuine concern. She said: 'It's a good day to cry, dear. It's a good day to cry.'

She wheeled me out of Recovery and down to my room. I remember her, as she said good-bye, taking my left hand and kissing it.

All these years, every time I went to St. Paul's Hospital, I instinctively searched for her. Today, there she was, sitting in Recovery talking with her colleagues. I wanted to thank her and tell her how much I appreciated all that she had done for me back in 1994, but I didn't know whether to tell her in front of her colleagues, or take her off to the side.

I opted for the latter.

Her name is Iris. She was stunned that I remembered her.

I'm glad I had the opportunity to thank Iris and to find out her name. Too many times, people who impact our lives are never told.

*They deserve our attention and care, even if
all we do is smile and say hello and thank you.*

Something else was drawing me back to my journal. For the past two weeks I had been experiencing
severe pain in my chest and rib cage area whenever I
breathed deeply.

Since April (seven months before), I had been seeing a plastic surgeon in regard to a tissue expander. After mastectomy surgery, this expander was immediately
placed under the skin where my left breast had been. I
had been going to the plastic surgeon on a weekly/bi-
weekly basis to have the expander filled with a saline
solution. The idea was to gradually stretch the skin until it was at the point where the expander could be removed and a breast implant inserted in its place.

The choices for a woman following mastectomy
surgery are threefold: leave a space where your breast
once was; have an expander put in at the time of surgery in preparation for a permanent implant; or have
lengthy reconstruction surgery that involves removing
skin from the abdomen and building it into a breast-like
mass. For me this last choice was never an option.

After much deliberation, I opted for the implant.
My surgeon, Dr. G., was adamant that all her patients
with implants were very happy with them. Given my
age, she strongly urged me to go the implant route.

Just as I had done before choosing chemotherapy
regimens, I researched all I could about implants,
downloading information from a number of sources.

From material I got from Health Canada, I felt I knew what to expect in terms of the risks and benefits of implants. I felt I could trust their information enough to base my decision regarding an implant on it.

I spoke to women who had had implants and were happy with them. I also talked with women who had had mastectomies. Many now wished they had opted to have implants put in at the time of the mastectomy surgery because it would have spared them another surgical procedure.

My surgeon sent me to a plastic surgeon and once again all the risks were discussed.

All things considered, I felt I was making an informed decision. For me, the bottom line was that an implant would offer me the flexibility of being able to wear my clothes as if I still had two full breasts, and for no other reason. And so, for eight months now, I had had this foreign object in my chest. It was hard as a rock and after each expansion of 25 to 50 ml of saline solution, my chest felt tight as a drum. It was so tight it even restricted the movement of my left arm.

I endured the pain by reminding myself of Jesus's unconditional love each time I touched the hard, unnatural lump. I was determined to be patient and persevere. I would be persistent in prayer. I would be a messenger of hope...

The plastic surgeon knew about the discomfort. On my last visit, he removed two visits worth of fluid and I instantly felt better. He said the hardness was due to the fact that I was an over-healer and had formed scar tissue that needed to be cut in order for the skin expansion to continue. This severing of the scar tissue was a minor day surgery that would quickly get me back on track, he said, and relieve me of the pain I was experiencing.

I found the news very discouraging. After eight months of trying, without success, to expand the tissue, I was now facing another surgery and I had no alternative but to go.

The surgery was booked for December 4.

Saturday, December 1, 2001

> *Three days before surgery.*
> *Went to Mass at St. Mary's. In the sermon, the question was posed: 'Where do you want to be at the end of your life's journey?' After giving it some thought, my answer was: 'At the end of my life journey, I want to be embraced by God's love which makes loving here on earth a vehicle to achieving that end.'*
> *"It is in giving to all men that we receive."*

Tuesday, December 4, dawned bitterly cold. Preparing for surgery had become all too familiar.

At the hospital, the plastic surgeon did some drawing below the site of the expander. His intention, he said, was to relocate it lower down.

As I drifted back to consciousness after the surgery, I instinctively reached for my left breast area to check for the familiar mound made by the expander. To my astonishment, there was nothing there.

At first I thought I was still groggy from the anesthetic, but a few minutes later the plastic surgeon came by and confirmed to me and Roberto what we now suspected.

The bone density of my ribs was very weak, he said. In fact, my rib cage was so weak that he refused to put the expander back in. He went on to say the radiation therapy I had received in 1994 had diminished the bone density. "I would like you to see a chest specialist," he concluded.

I was filled with consternation. For eight months I'd had this rock strapped to my chest for no good reason? Worse, now that I was aware of it, I could feel right through the bandages that there was a huge depression in my chest.

I was living the mastectomy all over again, only this time, I would be faced daily with these visible ravages.

The plastic surgeon said he, too, was disappointed.

Great, I thought.

A zillion questions assailed me, but I put them aside for the moment. I needed to get away. I needed to go home.

Roberto looked dazed, as if someone had hit him over the head.

I asked for toast, telling Roberto the sooner I had something to eat, the sooner I could get up and go home.

The nurse was surprised to hear I was ready to go. She asked if I wanted a strong pain killer before I left.

I told her I was in no pain, and that I actually felt a lot better now that the expander was gone.

I didn't care. All I wanted to do was get home and go to sleep, which I did immediately after dinner. I slept for three hours.

When I awoke, I checked my e-mails and made some journal notes.

It was later that night, as I lay in bed fully awake, that the impact and implications of the day hit me with full force. Unlike the mastectomy surgery, this time I wanted to see what was under the bandages.

I looked, and for the first time I became fully aware of the disfigurement that the implant-gone-wrong had left. I had a hole in my chest into which my closed fist fit nicely.

I began to cry. Quietly, at first. Then in uncontrollable sobs. My tears ran down my face and wet the bedsheets.

Roberto reached for me. There were no words to describe how each of us was feeling.

Later, as Roberto slept, I prayed. My nightgown had a pocket over top of where my left breast used to be. When I finished praying, I put my rosary in the pocket. The new concave made a Christmas cradle for the rosary, I reflected, and the thought made me cry all over again.

I pray for God's mercy in my life. Jesus, I am

sorry You had to die so that we might be saved. I love You, Lord Jesus.

I drifted off to sleep for a few hours with the words of Isaiah 40:11 resonating in my mind: *'As a shepherd carries a lamb, I have carried you close to my heart.'*

At 3:15 a.m. I got up to use the washroom, then went back to bed. Now it was Mozart's 'Serenade in G' that played over and over in my head. I knew I might as well get up.

I headed for the computer to e-mail my family in Italy who were awaiting news about the surgery. As I typed a very heart-rending letter in the quiet hours of that early morning, I wished they were nearer.

I look disfigured and deformed, but I am ALIVE, and that is what counts...

In the morning, I had an appointment with the plastic surgeon. I was bursting with questions that needed answers. I asked my good friend, Connie, to go with me.

It was the first time I had ever requested someone to go with me to the doctor's office. I felt I needed Connie, who had 'been there; done that'. She had had mastectomy surgery and nothing further done.

The meeting with the plastic surgeon did not provide any new information other than taking off my bandages and glancing at the disfigurement beneath. I was still struggling to make sense of everything that had happened.

Physically, there was relief to have the intense pressure off my chest, but I was now having difficulty breathing deeply because my rib cage was so depressed it was pressing on my heart and lungs. It was a feeling I would have to get used to. It occurred to me that if the process of expansion had continued, it would eventually have fractured my ribs.

Connie was shocked when she saw what the expander had done to me. Once we were alone in the examination room, she put her arms around me. The look on her face said it all.

I dressed quickly and we left for a quiet place where we could talk.

Connie admitted that when I first told her of my decision to have an implant, she wanted to persuade me against it, but refrained because of our age differences. She thought because I was younger, the implant was important to me for psychological reasons as well as for physical appearance. She did not realize I only wanted the implant for the flexibility it would afford me in wearing my clothes.

She said, at one point prior to my mastectomy, she was tempted to call me over for a show-and-tell. Now, of course, she wished she had followed her gut instinct.

After a pensive morning together, we went our separate ways: Connie to a luncheon, me to St. Paul's Church to catch the noon Mass.

During Mass, I was overcome with the most amazing sense of closeness to God and a deep love for Him. It was dramatically different from the sad and melancholy emotions that had assailed me earlier.

Arriving home, I found Cristina had baked a cake and was making her famous chocolate chip cookies. In the background, some of her favourite classical music was playing. The fire in the fireplace added a cozy warmth. How good it was to be home. I felt very blessed.

I grabbed a couple of cookies and headed for the computer to document the day's events in my journal.

As it turned out, journaling was impossible because the phone kept ringing. Cristina said she had been taking calls for me all morning.

One of the calls was from Loretta, my sister-in-law in Italy. She seemed surprised that I was sounding so much at peace despite all that had taken place. She said she needed to hear my voice; my e-mail would not suffice.

"You can tell me the truth," she said. "You don't have to be brave."

I reassured her that I wasn't putting anything on, and that for the time being, all was well.

She asked how Rob and Cristina were dealing with my situation; again I declared that all was running smoothly.

No sooner had we said our good-byes than Rob walked in from school.

"Hi, Mom," he said. "How did your visit with the plastic surgeon go? You won't be needing any more surgery, will you, Mom?" I could hear the apprehension in his voice.

I assured him that I would not, and suggested he go and sample some of Cristina's delectable baking.

I overheard him in the kitchen telling his sister that he had been dubbed the Paleontology King because he got a 94% in his paleontology exam.

"Hey," I protested, "you should have told me that news right away."

I realized that breast cancer had done it again. Concern for me had robbed my children of savouring their moments of achievement. How I wish I could have protected them from a breast cancer diagnosis, but it was not to be.

I still remember the day of the aborted surgery when we came home and Roberto told the children: "They would not operate on your mother because her liver enzyme count was elevated."

Cristina did not say anything, but Rob remarked: "That means the disease might have spread, right?"

I heard Roberto reply: "Yes, that is correct."

In that moment, my heart was filled with anguish for my children and my husband. All my life I had tried to protect them, but this was beyond my control.

Dear Jesus, help us make it through this stretch of the journey.

Saturday, December 8, 2001

The last of the bandages came off while bathing. For eight months, I have had the expander covering my heart and I could not feel

the pulsating rhythm of life within me. The
deep concave in my chest has bared my heart.
In placing my fist in the hole, it feels as though
I have my heart in my hand.

Looking at myself in the mirror for the first time
without any bandages, I began to cry. The neat incision
from the mastectomy surgery was now a bunch of
folded skin that would need time to heal, and possibly,
some touch-up surgery. All I could do in the meantime
was unite all my concerns and anxieties at the foot of
Jesus's cross.

My mother suggested that I do a salt water bath for
the surgical area. I agreed it would be a good way to
keep the wound infection-free. I proceeded with the
saline bath, but as I focused fully on my lopsided body
and traced the folded skin with my fingers, I began to
sob. I pressed down, trying to feel the rib cage and actually became nauseous when I realized how far I had
to press down before I could find my concaved ribs.

Monday, December 10, 2001
12:28 in the morning

Getting used to the new me is going to
take some effort. More questions are begin-
ning to surface, and with each question comes
new realizations about how this could have
happened. I am trying to make logical sense
of the concaved area that used to be my left

breast. I cannot fathom why this large hole also includes the chest area directly above the removed breast.

I am notorious for delayed reactions. It is now six days since the surgery and I can't help thinking the plastic surgeon was irresponsible in ignoring the effects of radiation on the bones in my chest. What should I do?

From the very beginning I had noticed that the expander was placed very high on my left side. Too high, it seemed to me. On the day of the surgery, I remembered the nurse telling me the plastic surgeon intended to do a relocation.

"A what?" I asked.

"The expander is going to be repositioned," she said.

"But I've come here to have the scar tissue cut because it is impeding the expansion," I protested.

The nurse rolled her eyes, shrugged her shoulders, and said: "You'll have to discuss it with your surgeon."

When the plastic surgeon arrived, he did some drawings on my chest well below where the former expander had been and in line with my right breast.

"I thought the expander was too high," I said, "but you guys are supposed to know what you're doing, right?"

He did not answer, nor did his expression change.

Now, as I felt the cavernous hole that lined up higher than my arm pit, I wanted to scream: "This chest area should be flat." I had seen other women who had had mastectomy surgery and no further treatment; all they have is a neat incision on a flat chest area. They didn't look deformed.

I became so upset, I couldn't stop crying. I needed to find out why this had happened to me. I wanted to get the word out to other survivors. Most important, I wanted to deal with the issue decisively so it would not dominate my life.

I felt betrayed by the doctor I had trusted. For eight months, he had repeated the same thing to me: that I was a scar former and that expansion would take longer for me. Did it never occur to him, as a doctor, that an expander needs a strong base from which to push? Had he ever wondered what was going on, especially after the time when he removed two visits worth of fluid from the expander?

He knew my medical history. He knew I'd had both chemo and radiation treatments in 1994. Never once did he say that given my past history, an implant might be a risky proposition. In fact, prior to the mastectomy, in discussing all the risk factors surrounding implants, he apparently found nothing that would hinder me from having an implant.

What hurt most was that I only wanted the implant so I could wear my clothes. What a laugh! I would have been much further ahead just having the mastectomy surgery and forgetting about the rest. Now I would have to pay very close attention to my necklines for the rest of my life.

And another thing, why on earth had I agreed to have the surgery during the holiday season? Somehow I would have to put all this turmoil behind me until the festive season was over. I refused to let it spoil my family's Christmas.

As I wrote in my journal long into the night, I prayed for guidance and patience, but those early morning hours were some of the worst I had endured since the cancer journey began in 1994. Unfortunately, my son Rob came down in the middle of it and discovered me pounding on the computer. How I wished he could have been spared that; he had enough on his mind preparing for the midterm he was writing the following day.

I felt somewhat better the next day, but the trauma and shock of my new shape was a reality I could no longer escape.

The day brought a nice surprise, however. Before my day surgery, I had taken two pictures, 'Jesus the Divine Mercy' and 'Our Lady of Guadalupe', to the framers. Since it was the holiday season, the framers could not promise the pictures would be ready by Christmas. What a wonderful surprise it was when they called to say my pictures were ready. It was even more special that the day I picked them up was December 12, the feast day of the Madonna of Guadalupe. It seemed a joyous coincidence.

Mother Mary is very present in our home. I have the Madonna of Medjugorje, the Madonna of Guadalupe, Our Lady of Perpetual Help, Our Lady of Graces,

Raffaelo's Madonna, and Botticelli's Madonna. While in Italy in the summer of 2001, I came across a 6' x 10' print of Mary. I wanted to buy it, but when Roberto and I estimated the cost of framing it, we decided against the purchase. "Besides," Roberto exclaimed, "where would you put it? Our house is slowly turning into a church with your collection."

Wednesday, December 12, 2001

Roberto and I met with the plastic surgeon today. He had an intern with him. We were introduced.

When asked how I was doing, I replied: Given the circumstances, not very well. I proceeded to pull out a sheet of questions to which Roberto and I wanted answers or some explanations. Before we could even begin, the surgeon, in the presence of his intern, said: 'Don't ask me any questions. I don't have the answers.'

Roberto and I were caught totally off guard.

The surgical area was checked; the doctor asked me to make another appointment to see him. We left, not making any appointment. I know I will never see him again.

In our home, we often remind one another that where there's a will, there's a way. Despite my predicament, I was confident there was a way to reverse the damage to my body.

This was my situation: my ribs were caved in and putting pressure on my heart and lungs. Somehow, the bones needed to be pushed outward. One way to do that was through breathing exercises, and I knew I had the lungs for it.

I remembered a time when I was teaching at St. Frances Elementary School and our staff attended an in-service workshop with two other schools. One of the activities that day was to test each individual's lung capacity. I don't recall how that corresponded to teaching, but I do remember taking the test. It involved blowing into a tube which lifted a little ball in a container. The individual's lung capacity was measured by how high the little ball rose.

It was near the end of the afternoon when our school was invited to take the test. Standing in line waiting for my turn, I zeroed in on the ball and quietly commenced to find my centre. The six husky men on our staff were amused that *petite moi* would even want to try, especially since they had all failed to bring the ball to the top of the container. Naturally, that made me dig in my heels even more.

I continued to focus on my breathing and the ball.

When my turn came, I let my long hair fall around my face to give me some privacy as I drew a very deep breath. I blew the ball right up to the top of the container!

I still recall the amazement of the gentleman conducting the test. I was the only person who accomplished it. My male colleagues were baffled and wondered what I did in the way of exercising. The other females in the room were delighted.

From that experience, I knew I had strong lungs and that with hard work, they might be able to push my ribs, if not back into place, at least a little bit forward. In time, the pressure on my ribs did decrease and my arm movement became less impeded.

Sunday, December 16, 2001

> *Father Paul's sermon at Mass was timely and thought provoking. He told us we need to cultivate being patient. We need to realize that we can only build in God's time. The rest symbol in music is just as important as the notes. Both are essential to the totality of the musical piece.*
>
> *This was particularly relevant for me today. Dear Lord, I prayed, help me find reprieve, help me to refocus and settle my fears. I need to rest and heal physically before any decisions are made or acted upon. Let me concentrate on Christmas festivities.*

We celebrated the Christmas season joyfully, but the hole in my chest was a constant reminder of less happy thoughts and emotions just beneath the surface.

Thursday, February 7, 2002

> *Harbouring resentment and anger only hurts the one carrying it. I know I must come to terms with the dangling emotions with which I am left. I must also come to terms with a course of action that I may or may not wish to take.*

With that in mind, I made an appointment with Sister Mariette to have a Reiki treatment. Reiki means 'of the spirit'. I felt I needed my mind to be focused and my thinking clear.

Before proceeding with the treatment, Sister Mariette and I had a chat. I told her what had happened to me and how I felt it was important for me to forgive the plastic surgeon for the hole in my chest so that I could move forward with my life.

Sister Mariette made me comfortable and commenced with the treatment.

She placed her hands on my chest and without warning, I began to cry. My mind replayed a visit I'd had with the plastic surgeon in the spring of 2001. I was feeling very distraught because I had just learned that I had little over a week to decide whether or not to have chemotherapy again. When the plastic surgeon asked me how I was, I began to explain my dilemma. He cut me off abruptly.

"I don't need to know any of this," he said curtly. "It does not concern me."

How ironic, I thought. At our first meeting, he told me he was the doctor I would be seeing the most. Now my situation was of no concern to him?

Lying on the table brought the recollection of how desperately I had held back the tears that day and prayed for a quick conclusion to the visit.

Now it all came back in a flood and I could not suppress my tears. I asked God to take away the anger, frustration, and hurt that I felt. In my prayer, I asked that I might find it in my heart to forgive the plastic surgeon. I prayed that this would never happen to any other female patient of his.

Why had I not asked to be seen by another plastic surgeon? Why hadn't I followed my gut instinct?

"Let it go," Mariette whispered, "let it all out..."

And I did.

Eventually, the sobs subsided. My body relaxed. I felt in perfect equilibrium.

I began to pray the Chaplet of Mercy and sank deeper and deeper into a calm, relaxed state. For weeks I had seen no imagery when I prayed, but as I completed the Chaplet and began to pray the rosary, using my fingers as counting beads, I was mentally transported to my safe place where I was greeted by my Inner Guide. I was afraid my mind would wander and prevent the imagery, but a strong sensation of well-being washed over me.

I was transported down the ten concrete steps. At the bottom, Happy quickly transformed into Jesus. Mary was with Him. They beckoned to me to come forward. I gave my left hand to Jesus and my right hand to Mary and the three of us walked together down the familiar gravel road.

At the fork, we turned left.

In the chapel, Jesus and Mary led me to a long winding staircase behind the free-standing cross. I had seen the staircase before in my imagery, but had always been reluctant to climb the stairs. Instead, I would open my eyes and come out of my meditative state. Today, I climbed the long staircase with Mary. Jesus remained at the bottom.

When we reached the top, I saw glimpses of faces of family members who had died. The first face I saw was my father's. He was smiling and looking very content. It struck me as odd that all these people were on my left. I saw nothing on my right.

Suddenly, I felt a strong Presence, a Light. All the people moved behind the Light and I was left standing alone in the presence of the Light, but I was not afraid.

I turned to find Mary waiting for me. Together, we walked down the stairs and back into the chapel where we met Jesus, and the three of us proceeded outside. We walked through the forest and back to the entry point where I left them and climbed the ten steps out of the meditation.

I opened my eyes to hear Sister Mariette telling me I could get up whenever I wanted. I was feeling so relaxed and light-headed after the treatment that she had to caution me to be careful driving home.

March 14, 2002

Finally! Better late than never! I've found the information I've been looking for. In the National Library of Medicine (NLM) it states that women who have previously had radiation therapy are poor candidates for breast implants because of a weakened chest wall. 'Reconstruction failure is significantly associated with the use of radiotherapy.'

If only I had discovered it sooner. Why was this not included in Health Canada's information outlining the risk of expander/implants for women? It would definitely have deterred me from going ahead with the procedure.

The information I accessed through Health Canada's 'It's Your Health' was extremely critical and influential in my decision-making process. I believed their report was up-to-date and non-biased.

Once more, in the midst of my frustration, I realized I was being given an opportunity to make lemonade out of the sour fruit I had been handed. I determined that I would indeed take positive action to make sure my anguish was not in vain. No other woman should have to go through what I had.

I started with Health Canada. After a number of calls, I managed to speak with someone who knew the person in charge of the information that is printed and circulated in regard to implant surgery. I gave him the relevant Internet address which he accessed while talking to me on the phone.

He agreed with me that if a female relative of his were in this position, he would want this important information to be available to her. He said Health Canada's information is constantly being updated and revised, and that after hearing my story, he would certainly relay the facts to the right people. I was told to expect a call from the person at Health Canada responsible for information regarding the benefits and the risks of implants.

No one called, so finally I tracked the person down. She told me that a companion, or mirror piece, to 'It's Your Health' was being written. I requested that it include, preferably at the top of the risk list, a line stating that women who have had radiation treatments are poor candidates for implants. I also suggested that she list the National Library of Medicine (NLM) website as a further information source.

The woman agreed to bring my concerns forward and said she would be happy to send me a draft of the companion piece to scrutinize and return.

I have not heard from her since.

In the middle of all this, it occurred to me that if I had access to this information, so did my plastic surgeon. Shouldn't he have known about this research? Was it not his business to know? Was it not his business to be up-to-date and well-informed?

And my oncologist. She knew I had decided to have an implant. Should she not have known the risks related to the radiation therapy I'd had?

In each case, one vital bit of information from the National Library of Medicine had been overlooked or forgotten: women who have previously had radiation therapy are poor candidates for breast implants because their chest walls may be weakened.

Armed with the NLM information, I made an appointment to see the Education Director of the Cancer Clinic. She promised to meet with the radiology department in the hope of making the information readily available to all female patients. Copies were also made for the oncologists on staff.

I put some copies in an envelope for my own surgeon, Dr. G., and asked her to share them with her colleagues.

And last, but certainly not least, I prepared an envelope full of information, along with a personal note, and delivered them to the plastic surgeon.

When I left his office that sunny April afternoon five months later, I knew I had let my resentment go. It had not happened overnight. Learning to forgive is a difficult task.

From time to time, when I think of the plastic surgeon, I whisper a prayer for him.

CHAPTER NINE

In November of 2001, we began making plans to go home to Padova, Italy, for a visit. We decided the visit would be from May 2 to June 2, 2002. Roberto's mother was not well and when we heard she had suffered a stroke, we were glad our tickets were already booked and preparations were underway.

Our son Rob would be staying behind to take Calculus at Intercession and Summer School, but Cristina was going with us. For the past year, she and I had been praying to the Madonna of Medjugorje, so both of us wanted to go and visit the shrine there.

More than twenty million pilgrims have visited Medjugorje in the past twenty years, making it a major world centre of prayer. Cristina and I wanted to present our own special intentions at the shrine of Mother Mary.

Friday, May 3, 2002

Arriving in Italy, the familiar sights and smells titillate my senses. Italy is an emotion.

The view from our bedroom is lush and verdant. Palm trees sway gently in the rain. I am embraced by intense satisfaction. It is good to be home.

We are happy to find Roberto's mother in a care home where she is well looked after. She had a tranquil look about her. At times, we are sure, if only briefly, she recognizes us.

On Sunday, after Mass, we were surprised to find the whole family gathered for a reunion. Everyone wanted to be brought up to speed. We spent a pleasant day doing that.

The following week we toured around Padova and did some travelling with my sister-in-law Marisa and her husband Carlo.

Before we left Saskatoon, I had purchased a new rosary. It was identical to the one that had changed colour when Carmen prayed for me. I bought it so I could show people the obvious and dramatic difference between the two.

On a day trip to Teolo with Marisa and Carlo, while we were visiting an 11th Century chapel, I had the impulse to show Marisa the two rosaries which I carried with me. I pulled them out of my purse. I held one rosary in each hand and began telling her how they both started out exactly the same, and how one had changed colour after a woman prayed for me when I was sick.

Marisa was astounded. She picked up the rosaries

and examined them both. It was an opportunity to tell her about the events of the past year and some of the amazing things that had taken place.

We were so engrossed in conversation that Carlo had to come and tell us that we were holding up the rest of the gang who were ready to embark on a hike into the forest.

Marisa showed the rosaries to Carlo.

"Both of them started out being like this one," she told him, "blue and silver linked."

"What do you mean they were both the same?" he responded. "One is definitely black and gold. The other is silver and blue."

I smiled at Carlo and confirmed that what his wife was telling him was true.

He led the way down the trail muttering to himself: "*Non è possibile. No way!*"

During that week, Marisa and I had many occasions to speak. Her home is directly above my mother-in-law's, where we were staying. She soon came to understand how anxious I was to go to Medjugorje, and why.

On one occasion, she exclaimed: "If all you have told me is true, how must we rearrange our lives?"

Saturday, May 11, 2002

Got up bright and early to pack for our trip to Medjugorje. Roberto's brother Nino and his wife Loretta will be travelling with us. The four of us and Cristina will go in Nino's Land Rover. We have been bugging him about having this huge vehicle in Italy; the fourteen-hour journey will be ample time for Nino to demonstrate its worthiness.

We decided, prior to leaving Padova, that we would travel through the interior of the former Yugoslavia for most of the trip. Our route enabled us to witness firsthand the ravages of the recent war. Everywhere, there were partially or totally demolished derelict houses and buildings. The desolation of this war-torn country was apparent and appalling at the same time. There was little evidence of life as we made our way to Medjugorje.

The last part of the journey was along the beautiful Adriatic Sea. The Adriatic coast was breathtaking, and the hustle and bustle of city life was in sharp contrast to the countryside.

We stopped in Split and found a hotel. After ten hours of driving, we were all ready for a rest. Tomorrow we would arrive in Medjugorje. After many months of anticipation, I could hardly wait for tomorrow to come.

"I want to show you great and marvelous things." Jeremiah 33:3

Sunday, May 12, 2002

I was pleased that we arrived in Med-jugorje on Sunday. The sky was pellucid. The sun was shining. What a great day!

Thank you, Jesus, for bringing us here. Thank You, Jesus, for all the good things in my life. I love You and I am sorry You had to die for us.

Our hotel was recommended by a priest Loretta knows. It was obvious why this hotel is frequented by cardinals, archbishops, bishops, and priests from all over the world. It was like a monastery on the inside, a place where one would go for a retreat.

Off the foyer was a chapel/grotto with three chairs facing a lovely altar. There were statues everywhere. The hotel exudes a peace and serenity conducive to spiritual renewal and prayer.

'Prayer is a powerful weapon, a key which opens the heart of God.'--Padre Pio

The hotel owner turned out to be a Italian-Canadian from Toronto. What a small world. We were greeted and asked which pasta he should make us for dinner.

While unpacking the vehicle and savouring our arrival, Loretta's cellular phone rang. It was her daughters, Elisa and Michela, calling to wish her a happy

Mother's Day. On vacation, it's hard to keep track of what day of the week it is, never mind special days. Cristina and I looked at one another and exchanged a hug and a smile. What a total, unexpected, unplanned, wonderful gift. How utterly serendipitous to arrive in Medjugorje on Mother's Day. I raised my arms to the heavens and toasted Our Mother: "Happy Mother's Day, dear Mary."

Loretta could not understand why we were both overcome with joy, but Cristina and I were revelling in the moment. We knew from here on, Mother's Day would have a new meaning for both of us.

Dinner was slated for 1:30 p.m. so we had two hours to freshen up and begin our tour of Medjugorje.

The church was a short distance from the hotel. We arrived for the last ten minutes of the Mass which was being said in English. It was filled to capacity.

The architectural style of the church inside and out was one of simple elegance. Aside from the sea of believers inside the building, what struck me most was the marvellous acoustics. The walls seemed to resonate with each musical note that was played or sung. The waves of sound encompassed my being as I knelt at the door.

"Thank you, dear Mother, for all your graces, especially for leading me closer to your son, Jesus."

After dinner we headed for the hill where the apparition of Mary appears. The weather was now overcast, and it was raining lightly. Umbrellas were distributed.

We split up, agreeing to meet at the top of the hill.

The path leading through the fields to Apparition Hill was a deep terracotta colour. Roberto, Cristina, and I made our way slowly to the foot of the hill. There weren't many people about at that time of day.

The climb was a challenging one. The hill is covered with an abundance of rocks in all shapes and sizes, making it more like an obstacle course.

We made our way carefully with me hanging onto Roberto. Cristina had ventured off on her own.

We encountered three women who were saying the Hail Mary in Italian. After we introduced ourselves, we asked if we could join them in praying. Franca, the lady leading the prayer, was from Calabria, Italy, my neck of the woods. Franca was very personable, and we soon got acquainted. I had my blue rosary in hand and Carmen's rosary in my pocket, and for some reason, I felt I wanted to show the three women both rosaries. I explained that both had once been the same colour.

They all thanked me sincerely for sharing this with them. Franca remarked: "*La Madonna è grande e fa tanti miracoli*--The Madonna is great and grants many miracles."

We continued to climb and pray, with Franca assisting her two older friends. The rain became persistent, but it did not deter the pilgrims. The rocks were hard to negotiate and the rain made it even harder, especially for the elderly. Soon we needed another break.

While we rested, Franca began to tell us why she was a devout believer. She directed her comments to

Roberto. I thought to myself: You've picked the right person. Roberto has been listening patiently and debating issues with me for the past year. Maybe Franca's comments will help give credibility to my own convictions. I knew Roberto was impressed by her obvious intelligence.

Franca's story was an amazing one. She is the head of a surgery unit in a Calabria hospital and described how she herself was in hospital with a head/brain injury. The doctors could not help her, so she turned to the Madonna of Medjugorje for help and she was healed. Franca is now in excellent health. This was her third visit to Medjugorje. She comes to give thanks for the healing she received.

We began climbing again. Near the top of Apparition Hill, with the shrine in sight, we said our good-byes and parted ways, each of us continuing in individual prayer. Cristina reached the shrine before we did. I could see her standing in the rain, praying on the turquoise rosary her Aunt Marisa had given her prior to leaving for Medjugorje. Cristina had noticed the iridescent rosary hanging in her grandmother's bedroom in Padova and asked if she could take it to Medjugorje. Aunt Marisa gave it gladly, declaring that Grandmother Luigia would be happy to know that someone was now praying on the rosary she loved so well.

I watched as Nino walked over to Cristina and sheltered her with his umbrella. It was raining quite heavily, but Cristina seemed oblivious, unaware even of her uncle's presence as she continued to pray.

The sight of my daughter in her black windbreaker with the hood pulled over her head, the turquoise rosary draped in front of her as she prayed on the beautiful beads, brought a lump to my throat.

At the shrine, an old lady who had climbed the hill with the aid of a long walking staff, put a rosary on the end of the staff which she lifted in order to place the rosary around the hand of the statue. Another woman had climbed the rocky hill barefoot.

At the top, I marvelled at the beauty of the surrounding countryside. I also spoke the intentions of my heart to Mother Mary and prayed for her intercession on behalf of my Special Friend.

On the way down, we encountered many groups led by guides making their way to the shrine. The hillside was now dotted with umbrellas as people picked their way over the treacherously wet rocks. One woman fell. I might have, too, had I not been hanging onto Roberto for dear life.

We met up with Franca again and stopped to chat. Franca said she was convinced the Madonna wanted us to meet. She gave me three medals and said that if we were planning to attend Evening Mass, we should go early in order to get a seat.

Roberto was captivated by this ebullient stranger who exuded such unwavering faith.

Franca left us with these words: *"Preparati per i miracoli possono succedere in qualsiasi momento*--Be prepared for miracles. They happen all the time."

It was the last we saw of her.

Roberto and I continued to make our way carefully down the hill. Cristina did not seem to be bothered by the wet boulders. She was hopping confidently from rock to rock. Normally, I would have been calling to her to be careful, but somehow, on this occasion, I knew she was protected.

We found her at the foot of the hill, waiting patiently.

The rain had left a wonderful freshness in the air, and we all enjoyed our walk back to the hotel.

> *Since arriving in Medjugorje, I have been praying on my new blue/silver-linked rosary. Frequently, I find myself checking it for any change in colour. I must be looking for a physical sign that the Madonna is listening to my prayers. I feel like a child awaiting a very special gift.*
>
> *I know if my rosary changes colour, it will be an indication to me that Mother Mary has heard my prayers for my Special Friend.*

That evening, Cristina and I went to church an hour early to find seats for all of us. On the way, my daughter confided: "You know, out there on the hill, when I was jumping from rock to rock? I had no fear of falling. I knew I would not fall."

The church was already full. All we could find was a place to stand behind the last pew. An elderly lady motioned for me to come and made room for me to sit next to her.

We chatted briefly; she was from England. I asked her if she knew in what language the Mass would be celebrated. She said she didn't know, but was hoping it would be either in English or German. As it turned out, the Mass was in Croatian with segments of the liturgy in English, German, Italian, and French. The language did not seem to matter. The acoustical sound of it filled my senses.

How utterly terrific it was to be here on Mother's Day.

Following Mass, we went to Nino and Loretta's room for a snack. We were the only five guests in the hotel. Roberto, Cristina, and I were on the third floor; Nino and Loretta were on the second.

The five of us reviewed the highlights of the day and in so doing, engaged in a lengthy dialogue about miracles versus modern science. Roberto seemed eager to share what he had heard from Franca. Loretta insisted it was important for me not to abandon modern science. I assured her I would continue to use whatever modern science had to offer.

I told her that it had become vital for me to harmonize and blend both the medical and spiritual aspects of healing. I had come to understand that God heals in many different ways. It may be through surgical procedures, through medications and treatments, through specific therapies, through prayer, or through any combination of the above.

I had also come to realize that the healing that

comes through prayer is not always physical. It may be spiritual or emotional healing, or take the form of inner peace, acceptance of circumstances, or blessings and graces received. Prayer yields many fruits regardless of whether there has been a physical healing or not.

Monday, May 13, 2002

> *In the early hours of the morning, while Roberto and Cristina packed, I made my way down to the chapel. There were no elevators. As I walked past Nino and Loretta's room, I could hear that they were also getting ready to leave.*
>
> *On the first floor, to the right of the stairs, there is a most haunting depiction of Christ crowned with thorns. I have been unable to walk by without stopping to stare at the image. It is black and white on some sort of cloth. Even now, I only have to close my eyes to re-capture the haunting gaze.*

Inside the chapel, I marvelled at the beautiful plants around the altar. There was a statue of Mary in front of a window that overlooks Apparition Hill. As the sun filtered through the glass, I brought all the prayer petitions of friends from Saskatoon to Our Mother.

I dug in my purse for Carmen's rosary, thinking I might have a better line to Our Mother on that rosary. I pulled out the new blue one instead and laid it on the chair next to some other items. For the first time since coming to Medjugorje, I did not check it for any change in color. Finding Carmen's rosary, I began to pray.

The memory of the Medjugorje experience would continue to replenish my well of faith.

"I love you, Dear Mother. Let me be worthy. Let love be my compass and guide in all that I do. Help me to make my life one of impact for God," I prayed. "Help me to make my life a marker for God. Let it be a Hip-Hip-Hooray for God!"

The Land Rover was loaded; we went for one last walk through Medjugorje. We revisited the church which was now empty, and said a final prayer of thanksgiving for the time spent in this quaint part of Bosnia. Then we were off.

It was a lovely sunny day. Loretta and Nino were in the front of the Land Rover; I was sitting in the back seat on the right-hand side. Cristina was in the middle seat with Roberto on her left.

Just prior to reaching the outskirts, I opened my purse and began fumbling around for something. I don't remember what. In the process, I accidentally pulled out my blue rosary which was entangled with some other objects.

When it came into my line of vision, my breath caught. I could not believe my eyes. Some of the silver links had started to change to gold.

I untangled the rosary and held it closer to the window. Was I mistaken? No, the beads, which had been a distinct blue shade, were now deeper blue in colour.

My heart began to race.

I gave the rosary to Cristina. She knew instantly what had happened. A satisfied smile curved her lips.

She handed the rosary to Roberto. He, too, knew what it had looked like. He was speechless.

I told Cristina I needed to show the rosary to Nino and Loretta, especially in view of the debate/discussion we'd had the previous evening about miracles and modern science. She was uncomfortable with the idea, but I said: "We are all on the same faith journey, just at different stages, but we are nonetheless on the same path. That's why it is imperative for us to share our experiences."

I could hardly wait until the Land-Rover stopped for some traffic lights. I handed the rosary to Nino.

Perplexed, he said: "This rosary is changing colour."

He gave it to Loretta. She did not comment.

I clasped the rosary tightly in my hands and ask Mother Mary to forgive any doubts I'd had. Earlier, in the chapel, I had not bothered to check or to pray on my blue rosary. I'd given up hope of it changing colour.

As we drove out of Medjugorje, I was infused with such an acute joy that I prayed the Chaplet of Mercy for anyone back home in Saskatoon who came to mind.

I kept the rosary in the palm of my hand for the entire trip to our next destination, Krk, and continued to be amazed by the string of beads that glittered in the sun. Surely this is how I must have felt when I opened my first Christmas gift, I thought.

Tuesday, May 14, 2002

> *Krk is a beautiful harbour city. Our stay was most enjoyable.*
> *The first thing I did when I awoke was to look at my rosary which was tucked under my pillow. I went out onto the balcony and examined the rosary in the bright sunlight. Yes, it was definitely undergoing a visible metamorphosis. My elation was indescribable.*

We arrived at Pula that evening. I sat at a patio table adding to my journal while the blue-green Adriatic Sea serenaded me. The rosary was on the table. I picked it up and once again was mesmerized by the transformation that was clearly taking place. Yes, indeed. All the Hail Mary links were more yellow now. Only the three links before and after the Our Father bead were still silver with no visible change.

> *Thank you, dear Mother, for being the key that leads us to Jesus. Thank you, Jesus. I am humbled, grateful, and very content.*

Wednesday, May 15, 2002

> *Roberto draws the drapes. Another glorious day. I feel like a child with a treasure. My rosary. My treasure.*

From the window, I can see a fishing boat being bombarded by seagulls looking for scraps to eat. Outside our patio, there is a planter filled with aromatic plants. I run my hands over lavender and rosemary. It's great to be alive.

Our last stop before reaching Italy was Postonia. There, we visited the magnificent caves and saw the wondrous sculptings of Mother Nature. The caves are spectacular beyond words. Throughout the trip, I continually wished Rob was with us, but that day I wished it more than ever. Mineralogy is his field of study. A book and some fossils would have to suffice until he could come and experience the caves for himself.

We were now on the last leg of our journey back to Italy. Croatia, Slovenia, and Bosnia had made lasting impressions on all of us, but for me, realizing my dream of visiting Medjugorje had far exceeded my fondest expectations.

Our last two weeks in Italy were spent sightseeing in parts of central Italy. We spent the final seven days in Padova with family and friends.

The crown jewel of Padova is the Basilica of St. Anthony. There, I abandoned myself in thanksgiving for a vacation that had played out like no other.

The first thing I did when we got home to Saskatoon was go and purchase another rosary identical to the one I took to Medjugorje. The one from Medjugorje continued to transform; the beads are now jet black and the links, a rich shiny gold. The new one, which I bought solely for comparison purposes, is still the way the other used to be, blue beads with silver links. At every opportunity, I share my Mary experience.

That same year, on December 8th, the feast day of the Immaculate Conception, I took the rosary to St. John Bosco Church where praying of the entire rosary, all four mysteries (twenty decades), was taking place. Carmen was to lead us in prayer.

I had made arrangements with Carmen to pray by proxy for the loved one of my friend Lucia. I suggested to Lucia that she join me for the afternoon rosary.

Afterward, I introduced Lucia to Carmen, and we all prayed for Lucia's brother.

On the way home, I felt an overwhelming need to make sure my rosary was in my purse. It was as though I had a premonition I was going to lose it. I asked Lucia to retrieve the purse from the back seat and look inside for the rosary.

"Yes," she remarked, "you wouldn't want to lose that special rosary you took to Medjugorje, would you?"

It was in my purse. I was greatly relieved.

That evening I attended the 8:00 p.m. Mass at St. Paul's Cathedral with another friend, Giovina. She wanted to talk to me, so after Mass we went to a restaurant for coffee.

Whenever possible, I like to pray the Chaplet of

Mercy at 3:00 p.m. because that is when Jesus died. Asking for His mercy at that exact time has become poignantly symbolic for me.

However, when I went to get my rosary out of my purse at 3:00 p.m. the next day, it was missing.

I recalled taking it out of my purse at Mass the night before. I remembered looking at it during Mass, fondling it, caressing the beads, marvelling at this special treasure, and being thankful. I also remembered placing the rosary in the pocket of my blazer after Mass.

I ran to the closet and checked my blazer. It was not there.

Feeling a rush of panic, I called to Rob and Cristina who were both home at the time. We all began searching the house.

I soon realized it was an exercise in futility because I distinctly remembered placing the rosary in the pocket of my blazer.

By now, I was very distressed and upset. Rob tried to say something to console me, but his sister snapped back: "You don't understand how much that rosary means to Mom."

Fighting for composure, I telephoned the Cathedral. The secretary said the janitor had already vacuumed and that if he had found the rosary, he would have brought it to the office. She could hear the desperation in my voice and offered to go and look for it in the church herself. I explained that I always sit directly in front of the statue of Mother Mary whenever I attend

Mass at St. Paul's. She said she would call me back.

In the meantime, I phoned the restaurant where Giovina and I had had coffee. The hostess obligingly searched the 'Lost and Found' box, but no rosary had been turned in. She said she would also check with the night shift when they arrived.

Roberto arrived home from work to find a very distraught wife trying to prepare an early dinner so he could go to his Monday Night tennis game which has been part of his routine for many years. Seeking to comfort me, he observed: "Maybe the person who found the rosary needs it more than you."

We sat down to dinner. I was not a happy camper.

During dinner, the secretary from the church phoned. She had found nothing. Even though it was not generally done, she offered to put a notice in the church bulletin. "This rosary is obviously very important to you," she said.

I thanked her for her kindness, but my heart was heavy.

After dinner, alone in the laundry room, I bemoaned my loss aloud to God. "Fine," I told Him with unhappy tears in my eyes, "if someone needs that rosary more than I do, so be it. But, boy, will I cry myself to sleep tonight!"

No sooner had I uttered those sentiments than, all of a sudden, I was infused with a heat that rushed from my toes to my head. At the same instant, the telephone rang. I knew even before I answered that the restaurant was calling to say they had found my rosary.

I was right. The rosary had been found. The night before, the waitress, sensing it was something precious to someone, had stored it in a different place.

My joy was unconstrained. I quickly wrote a thank you note, wrapped up a box of chocolates for the restaurant staff, and rushed over to get my rosary.

My life was at another crossroad. I had spent months recording my remarkable experiences in my journal. I had thoughts of putting everything into book form, but now I was struggling with other questions: do I want to make myself vulnerable and expose my intimate story? Should I put it into a book? Would anyone want to read of my experiences? And even more important, would anyone benefit from reading such a book?

Ultimately, the decision was taken out of my hands.

In February of 2003, just before Valentine's Day, Judy, my friend of many years, came to visit. We had not seen each other for several weeks.

I was looking forward to Judy's visit. She always manages to put a new spin on any given situation. Over the years, when tackling different issues, I have come to rely on her quiet, calm, but strong demeanour.

We visited happily for a while, then she said:

"So when are you going to publish your book?"

"It's a long story," I responded and redirected the conversation.

A half hour passed. Judy asked again. "What's up with the book?"

I dug out the pages of manuscript I had printed off, opened it randomly, and began to read aloud. It was the first time I had held and read from my hard copy. I could hardly believe what I heard myself reading. Out of the hundred typewritten sheets, the page I picked out of the stack was the one describing the events of March 8, 2001.

I had just repeated that same story earlier to friends at my mother's home.

"*La Madonna mi mandò lo Spirito Santo quel mattino*--Mother Mary sent the Holy Spirit to me that morning," I told them. I had never expressed this belief and emotion in my Italian dialect before. Somehow, when I did, all that had happened to me took on an even deeper meaning.

To relive the most important element of my story twice in one day? This could not be a coincidence.

When I finished reading, I was surprised to see tears in Judy's eyes.

"Do whatever you have to, Francesca, but you must put this in a book. Do it. Find a way!"

My impetus to move forward with the project was further reinforced a couple of days later through a telephone conversation with Carmen. The e-mail Carmen sent after our heart-to-heart on the phone describes the last vision she gave me:

"Francesca phoned me on February 15, 2003, shortly after lunch. She was very tired and anxious about publishing this book. Her

mind was full of runaway thoughts as to how to do this. She hadn't slept and I could hear the fatigue in her voice. As I prayed for peace in her heart, I experienced a few visions...

#1 I saw Jesus and Francesca walking on a path, Jesus was leading the way, being very patient with her, waiting for her to catch up.

#2 I saw Francesca wrapped in a baby blanket. Mary was holding her.

#3 I saw her book, also wrapped in a blue blanket, in the arms of Mary.

#4 I saw blue dominos, one falling into the other. The dominos changed into books. (I was under the impression that this book cover was going to be pink. I was so surprised to see blue books.) There were many books. Each person who read her book experienced an increase in faith, having being inspired by the Holy Spirit.

I also felt that the vulnerability she feels about opening up her very personal feelings and sharing them with everyone would be turned to peace of mind and heart...Thanks Be To God!!!"

In sending me this e-mail, Carmen confirmed what I already knew: that this was not my story. It was Mary's story--a story that leads us to Her son, Jesus. And it was a story that had to be shared.

I told Carmen that my intention from the very beginning was to have a blue cover for my book, if there was to be one.

Initially, the whole concept of being healed was too great for me to fathom, comprehend, or internalize. So I placed the memory of March 8 in a box and stored it away for another day--yet another day--and yet another day. When I was finally able to look inside the box, the stark truth and realization of what had taken place on that March morning was completely overwhelming. I could no longer deny the truth that was exploding from inside the box.

I want to shout from the highest mountain that on March 8, 2001, early on the morning of my liver ultra-sound, the intercession of our dear Mother Mary brought the Spirit of her Son, Jesus, to me. The power of God's Holy Spirit touched my body and with His Boundless Love, bathed it with a heat that healed every molecule, every atom, every cell of my being.

My heart is bursting with responsibility, yet full of joy because I have now released the beautiful miracle that defies what we humans call logic. The dance be-tween my heart and mind has ended, leaving me with only sweet refrains. My logical mind no longer over-powers my heart. I have learned to think more with my heart, and in doing so, gut instinct has become what I fondly call God instinct.

My life 'NPink has been enriched by Jesus's un-failing presence. I can never repay Him.

Without doubt or reservation, March 8, 2001 has

left an indelible mark of God's handiwork at play in my life.

"Not by power, not by might, but by My Spirit, says the Lord." Zechariah 4:6.

I have come to realize with great sadness that I will probably never again experience that all-consuming, blissful, electrifying, deliberate surge of warmth I felt on that morning, but the grandeur and rapture of that day is never far from my mind and spirit.

From time to time, I still receive the occasional 'rush of heat'. I believe the uncharacteristic warmth is God tapping me on the shoulder, reminding me of His constant presence and love.

I often wondered why, on March 8, I experienced the incredible, specific heat after praying the first four decades, but not after the fifth. It was only recently, while praying and meditating, that the answer came. It was like a voice speaking clearly in my head: "The job was done. You were healed."

When we are a witness to any event firsthand, a choice must be made: to report with a truthful, open heart what was witnessed, or to do a 'hit and run'. I now feel I have done my part-- to be a truthful witness.

Jesus challenges us to pay our dues and speak out with truth and conviction, even at the risk of being ridiculed. Each of us is challenged to be a witness for Christ.

Fear is our greatest obstacle. Fear is how the devil (I can now finally write the word without any fear) controls us. The only fear I now have is the fear of offending God. I will not be debilitated by fear. My spirit will not be dulled by fear.

Dante, in the Divine Comedy, states it best. The hottest places in hell are reserved for those of us who insist on remaining neutral in times when we are challenged to speak out. Well, I am speaking out. I am stepping out in faith and acknowledging that two wondrous, stupendous miracles have been witnessed. One by me alone on the morning of March 8, 2001; the other on May 13 of 2002 as the five of us were leaving Medjugorje.

Love is the engine that should drive humanity. Love is the food of life. In love and without reservation, I have reported what I have witnessed.

"What God has opened, no one can close. What God has closed, no one can open." Rev 3:7

FINAL REFLECTIONS 'NPINK

My journey *'NPink* which began in 1994 has made me realize the immense power of the human spirit that dwells in each one of us. I have no regrets. This cancer journey has taken me physically, emotionally, and mentally to places I could never have imagined. Breast cancer has allowed me to look at my life through pink-tinted glasses; the radiant glow enables me to embrace with gratitude the life God has given me.

I have been on a continuum of spiritual evolvement.

I know without any doubt that the events of the past months have challenged me to rethink what my relationship to God should be. In a world gone technologically mad, I have found the umbilical cord that connects with our Creator. It is easy to miss the human element in the rush of everyday living. We need to become more human-full. We need to become more God-full.

My journey *'NPink* has led me to many wonderful people. I am especially blessed to have met Carmen.

She is a holy woman and visionary with unsurpassed faith. I am awed and inspired by her faith and steadfast commitment to God.

People often ask: "If you could go back, would you change anything?" My response is a heartfelt: No. The cancer experience awakened in me the reality of what I had always known to be true. We have the power to think and choose. That gives us control over how we respond to life. As a result, my cup will continue to be full. Cancer can never take away my ability to love which is the balm of true living.

Psalm 90 sums up where I am today: "*In You, O God, my refuge I take; I will not be afraid.*"

In a perfect world, it would be super-fantastic if doctors and patients prayed together or for each other, prior to surgery, for instance. Total healing can only take place when there is a blending of the spirit, the mind, and the body. Combining science and religion/spirituality could become a revolutionary pinnacle of achievement for humanity. WOW!!

From 1994 to 1999, I was privileged to speak to many groups from the Girl Guide Convention to the Insurance Association, Law Society, churches, and schools. I always ended my presentations with my favourite quote from the Bible: "*I have come that you might live life and live it to the full.*"

God's gift to us is our life. How we live that life is our gift back to God.

When I visit my father's grave, I often wander among the gravestones, reading the names and dates.

The dates of birth and death are always linked with a dash. For me, the dash is all-important. It represents our life.

God gently watches as we struggle to make that dash count, to make it stand for something which, in the end, may help us to justify our existence.

My quest now is to justify my existence--my dash, my life--here on earth in God's time.

For all people, especially those who live with adversity, may they soar on the wings of faith, hope, and God's infinite love,

Butterfly,
Francesca Iosca-Pagnin.

P.S. I have also witnessed the on-going healing of my Special Friend. Through baseline medication combined with cranio-sacro and visceral manipulation therapy, my Special Friend has made an amazing recovery.

Thank you, Jesus.

PRAYING THE ROSARY

For more than nine hundred years, the rosary has been a religious tool for prayer. By the 12th Century, it was already common practice to use beads to count certain repeated prayers. Christian monks ran beads or knotted string through their fingers as they chanted their 150 required Psalms.

Each of the constituent prayers of the rosary, the Apostles' Creed, the Lord's Prayer, the Hail Mary, and

How to Pray the Rosary

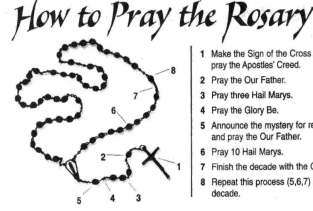

1 Make the Sign of the Cross and pray the Apostles' Creed.

2 Pray the Our Father.

3 Pray three Hail Marys.

4 Pray the Glory Be.

5 Announce the mystery for reflection and pray the Our Father.

6 Pray 10 Hail Marys.

7 Finish the decade with the Glory Be.

8 Repeat this process (5,6,7) for each decade.

the Glory Be, is rooted directly or indirectly in the Gospels.

It was Pope Pius V who instituted the familiar form of the rosary and recommended Catholics pray on their beads while reflecting on the life of Christ. He encouraged praying 150 Hail Marys (from Luke 1:28 & 42) in decades separated by an 'Our Father' (universally known as The Lord's Prayer).

I derived great comfort and encouragement from contacting the Upper Room Living Prayer Centre. It can be reached at 1-800-251-2468 any time of the day or night.

For more information on craniosacral and visceral manipulation therapy, contact the Upledger Institute of Florida at 1-800-233-5880 or http://www.iahp.com.

The National Library of Medicine website: http://www.nlm.nih.gov.

Please visit my website: http://www.reflectionsinpink.com.

Additional *Reflections 'NPink* books and pins are available through: http://www.anthopio.com.